# Using
# Visual Basic

# Books Available

## By the same authors:

BP546   Microsoft Works Suite 2004 explained
BP545   Paint Shop Pro 8 explained
BP544   Microsoft Office 2003 explained
BP538   Windows XP for Beginners*
BP525   Controlling Windows XP the easy way*
BP522   Microsoft Works Suite 2002 explained
BP514   Windows XP explained*
BP513   IE 6 and Outlook Express 6 explained*
BP512   Microsoft Access 2002 explained
BP511   Microsoft Excel 2002 explained
BP510   Microsoft Word 2002 explained
BP509   Microsoft Office XP explained
BP498   Using Visual Basic
BP493   Windows Me explained*
BP491   Windows 2000 explained*
BP487   Quicken 2000 UK explained*
BP486   Using Linux the easy way*
BP465   Lotus SmartSuite Millennium explained
BP433   Your own Web site on the Internet
BP341   MS-DOS explained
BP284   Programming in QuickBASIC
BP258   Learning to Program in C

If you would like to purchase a Companion Disc for any of the listed books by the same authors, apart from the ones marked with an asterisk, containing the file/program listings which appear in them, then fill in the form at the back of the book and send it to Phil Oliver at the stipulated address.

# Using
# Visual Basic

## by

## P.R.M. Oliver
## and
## N. Kantaris

**Bernard Babani (publishing) Ltd**
**The Grampians**
**Shepherds Bush Road**
**London W6 7NF**
**England**
*www.babanibooks.com*

# Please Note

Although every care has been taken with the production of this book to ensure that any projects, designs, modifications and/or programs, etc., contained herewith, operate in a correct and safe manner and also that any components specified are normally available in Great Britain, the Publishers and Author(s) do not accept responsibility in any way for the failure (including fault in design) of any project, design, modification or program to work correctly or to cause damage to any equipment that it may be connected to or used in conjunction with, or in respect of any other damage or injury that may be so caused, nor do the Publishers accept responsibility in any way for the failure to obtain specified components.

Notice is also given that if equipment that is still under warranty is modified in any way or used or connected with home-built equipment then that warranty may be void.

© 2001 BERNARD BABANI (publishing) LTD

First Published - February 2001
Reprinted - June 2001
Reprinted - November 2001
Reprinted - December 2001
Reprinted - April 2002
Reprinted - August 2002
Reprinted - December 2002
Reprinted - July 2003
Reprinted - March 2004
Reprinted - February 2005

British Library Cataloguing in Publication Data:

A catalogue record for this book is available from the British Library

ISBN 0 85934 498 3

Cover Design by Gregor Arthur
Printed and Bound in Great Britain by Cox & Wyman

# Preface

Visual BASIC has become the most popular 'dialect' of BASIC in use today on IBM and compatible computers. The original version of BASIC (which stands for Beginner's All-purpose Symbolic Instruction Code) was first developed as a teaching language at Dartmouth College in 1964. In 1978 a 'standard BASIC' was adopted as a result of recommendations on the minimum requirements of the language.

BASICA, written by Microsoft for use with the IBM PCs, and GWBASIC (its equivalent form running on compatibles), was an enhanced version of standard BASIC, embodying nearly 200 commands. These were bundled with pre-DOS 5 versions of the operating system, but users of MS-DOS 5 and higher had access to a cut-down version of Microsoft's QuickBASIC, known as QBASIC.

QuickBASIC was Microsoft's first *compiled* version of BASIC, the earlier ones being *interpreted* languages. With an interpreted language each and every statement of code has to be interpreted by a separate program called the interpreter before the program is actually run. This happens each time a statement is encountered, even if it appears within a loop. With a compiled language, on the other hand, a separate program, called the compiler, is used to check the whole program for errors and then compiles it into the machine specific code that will actually be executed by the computer at run time. Statements within loops are only checked once, which makes a compiled program far more efficient than an interpreted one.

Visual BASIC is now very different from these early versions. It is an event driven, or Object Oriented, compiled language that uses all of Windows' visual features. It also includes most of the features built into QuickBASIC, so earlier programs can be easily adapted to run on Visual Basic. As well as being a stand-alone Windows 'programming environment', a slightly modified version of Visual Basic is also included with Microsoft Office applications as VBA, or Visual Basic for Applications.

# About this Book

*Using Visual Basic* is loosely based on our earlier book, *Programming in Visual BASIC for Windows,* and is a guide to programming in a Windows environment using Microsoft's Visual Basic. For this book we used Version 6.0 of Visual Basic, on a PC running under Windows *Me*. The reader is not expected to have any familiarity with the language as both the environment and statements are introduced and explained with the help of simple programs. The user is encouraged to build these, save them, and keep improving them as more complex language statements and commands are encountered.

The very size of Visual Basic and its programming environment, can be very daunting to a new user, so this systematic approach should make learning very much easier.

The first three Chapters give an overview of Visual Basic and the graphic based environment it uses. Forms and the more simple controls that go with them are introduced, but no attempt is made to explain how to use Microsoft Windows itself. It is assumed that if you want to create programs that work with Windows, you will be familiar with the interface itself. If you do need to know more about the Windows environment, then we suggest you select an appropriate book from the 'Books Available' list - these are all published by BERNARD BABANI (publishing) Ltd.

Chapters 4-7 cover the programming language and how it is entered into your PC, dealing with the basic Visual Basic statements which control program flow, input and output, and leading to the concepts of strings and arrays.

In Chapter 8 we return to some of the more powerful intrinsic Visual Basic controls that allow you to produce the sort of Windows programs that you can buy. The next chapter covers functions and procedures which expand the programming capabilities of the user beyond the beginner's level. Chapter 10 deals entirely with disc file handling techniques and should be of special interest to those who need to process large quantities of data. The two main types of data files are discussed in some detail, namely, sequential and random access types. How to easily use the Windows file handling procedures is also covered.

A chapter then introduces how Visual Basic can interact with Microsoft's Office applications, Word, Excel, and the database Access.

The last chapter gives an overview of the powerful debugging features of the program, and describes how to create, compile and package your application programs with the Visual Basic wizards.

A glossary of mainly Visual Basic terms is included, which should be used with the text where necessary. For reference purposes, appendices also detail the Visual Basic naming conventions, user-defined formats, event procedures and main keyword listings and descriptions.

Like the rest of our computer series, this book was written with the busy person in mind. It is not necessary to learn all there is to know about a subject, when reading a few selected pages can usually do the same thing quite adequately. Using this book, it is hoped that you will be able to come to terms with Visual Basic and start producing programs of your own in the shortest possible time. Good luck and enjoy yourself, because it can be fun.

If you would like to purchase a Companion Disc for any of our books listed on page ii, **apart from those marked with an asterisk**, containing the file/program listings which appear in them, then fill in the form at the back of the book and send it to Phil Oliver at the address given.

# About the Authors

**Phil Oliver** graduated in Mining Engineering at Camborne School of Mines in 1967 and since then has specialised in most aspects of surface mining technology, with a particular emphasis on computer related techniques. He has worked in Guyana, Canada, several Middle Eastern and Central Asian countries, South Africa and the United Kingdom, on such diverse projects as: the planning and management of bauxite, iron, gold and coal mines; rock excavation contracting in the UK; international mining equipment sales and international mine consulting. In 1988 he took up a lecturing position at Camborne School of Mines (part of Exeter University) in Surface Mining and Management. He retired from full-time lecturing in 1998, to spend more time writing, consulting, and developing Web sites.

**Noel Kantaris** graduated in Electrical Engineering at Bristol University and after spending three years in the Electronics Industry in London, took up a Tutorship in Physics at the University of Queensland. Research interests in Ionospheric Physics, led to the degrees of M.E. in Electronics and Ph.D. in Physics. On return to the UK, he took up a Post-Doctoral Research Fellowship in Radio Physics at the University of Leicester, and then in 1973 a lecturing position in Engineering at the Camborne School of Mines, Cornwall, (part of Exeter University), where between 1978 and 1997 he was also the CSM Computing Manager. At present he is IT Director of FFC Ltd.

# Acknowledgements

We would like to thank both Microsoft UK and AUGUST.ONE Communications Ltd for kindly providing the software that was used to produce this book.

# Trademarks

**Arial** and **Times New Roman** are registered trademarks of The Monotype Corporation plc.

**HP and LaserJet** are registered trademarks of Hewlett Packard Corporation.

**IBM** is a registered trademark of International Business Machines, Inc.

**Intel** is a registered trademark of Intel Corporation.

**Microsoft, MSDN, MS-DOS, Windows, Windows NT, Visual Basic** and **Visual Studio**, are either registered trademarks or trademarks of Microsoft Corporation.

**PostScript** is a registered trademark of Adobe Systems Incorporated.

All other brand and product names used in the book are recognised as trademarks, or registered trademarks, of their respective companies.

# Contents

# 1

## Package Overview

Visual Basic lets you create your own programs or applications, for running yourself, or for running on other peoples PCs. The applications you create can be as simple or as complex as you like, and can even be used for such things as, manipulating databases, files, the Internet or almost anything else you want it to do!

Visual Basic, unlike other structured languages such as its predecessor QuickBASIC or C, is an *event driven* programming language. Instead of the program flow being controlled from the written code and running mainly from the first to the last lines of code, it is controlled by interactive events at run-time, such as the clicking of a mouse on a button or form. When such an event occurs, the program code attached to that event is actioned. Buttons, forms, controls, the screen and your printer, etc., are all considered as *objects* and Visual Basic is known as an Object Oriented language. It reacts to the manipulation of objects. Once this concept is grasped, the change from other programming languages is much easier.

While you are building your application you can 'run' it from within Visual Basic to make sure it works properly. When you are completely happy with it you can then compile and package your program into an executable form that anyone else can then run on their Windows based PC. In fact, if it is good enough, you can even distribute your application royalty-free, as long as you have registered your copy of Visual Basic.

One catch, though, with using Visual Basic to develop programs is that other users of your applications will require the MSVBVM60.DLL file, and possibly others (depending on which controls you have used), to run your program. At some 1.3MB, this file is quite large and can be a setback when you want to distribute your program on the Internet, or on a floppy disc.

# Editions of Visual Basic

Since the original Visual Basic for Windows was released in May 1991 there have been several updates and improvements to the package, the major jump being from 16 bit to 32 bit which took place with Visual Basic 5.0.

## Visual Basic 6.0

At the time of writing, Version 6.0 was the current version. This, like its predecessors, comes in several Editions.

The **Working Model** is sometimes distributed 'free of charge' with the more expensive Visual Basic books. It is a 'cut down' version that allows you to experiment with the program, but does not allow you to create your own executable '.exe' files.

The **Learning Edition** is the simplest and cheapest version, coming with the standard Visual Basic controls and allowing the creation of executable '.exe' files from the code.

The **Professional Edition** comes with many more features and ActiveX controls to supplement the standard ones, and costs quite a bit more.

The **Enterprise Edition** is the top one, and is mainly for programmers who are creating applications for servers and networks. It costs several hundred pounds more.

To complicate matters further, as well as providing 'stand alone' editions of Visual basic, Microsoft also produce a similar range of **Visual Studio** editions. These are like development compendium packages and all contain Visual Basic as well as other development tools such as Visual C++, Visual J++ and Visual FoxPro. For anybody who needs to get serious about developing very 'heavy' Windows applications these may be the best way to go.

If you are a student, a teacher or an academic there is also a **Students Edition**. This is a Professional version of Visual Studio sold at a very low cost to students (anyone working towards a recognised qualification) and teachers. If you qualify, this is definitely the version to get!

For most people, the Professional Edition is probably the best option, as long as you are happy with the initial cost. While updating this book we started off with the Students Edition and then replaced it with the Enterprise Edition of Visual Studio. You will find, however, that most of our examples are pretty simple, so the book can be used equally with all of the flavours of Visual Basic.

## VB Script

VB Script is a simplified version of Visual Basic which is used in Web pages. It has the major disadvantage that it is only supported by Microsoft's Internet Explorer 4 browser or later.

### Visual Basic for Applications

VBA is a slightly different edition of Visual Basic, which comes with most of Microsoft's Office applications, such as Word, Excel, etc. The basic program functions are the same, but it is customised for the particular application being used.

## Installing Visual Basic

Whatever edition you have, the initial installation procedure is very well automated, but before you start, make sure your system is suitable.

### System Requirements

Microsoft specify the following minimum set-up. An IBM compatible PC with a 486DX/66 MHz or higher processor (or any Alpha processor running Microsoft Windows NT Workstation, or higher); a hard disc with at least 120MB of spare room, 16 MB of RAM for Windows 95, 32 MB of RAM for Windows NT Workstation, a mouse, a VGA or higher-resolution screen display and a CD-ROM disc drive. This should be running Microsoft Windows 95 or later, or Microsoft Windows NT Workstation 4.0 (Service Pack 3 recommended) or later.

To make use of the advantages of the Windows interface, however, we would recommend the most powerful Pentium PC you can get your hands on!

## The Installation Process

The exact installation process will depend on which edition of the program you have. With Windows open and no other programs running, place the first CD into the CD-ROM drive, with us this was the Visual Studio 6.0 Disc 1. The Setup program may well start automatically, if not, click the **Start** button on the Windows task bar, select **Run**, type **e:\setup.exe** in the **Open** text box, as shown in Fig. 1.1, and click on **OK**. If your CD-ROM drive is not the E: drive, you should obviously use the correct drive letter instead.

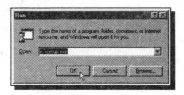

Fig. 1.1 Using the Windows Run Box

It's then just a case of following the instructions given. You will be stepped through the procedures of accepting Microsoft's License agreement and of entering the Product ID number. This number should be shown as the 'CD Key' on the back of your original CD box. When asked, opt for a customised installation so that you can select what is actually placed on your hard disc.

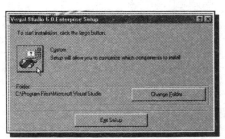

Fig. 1.2 A Custom Installation

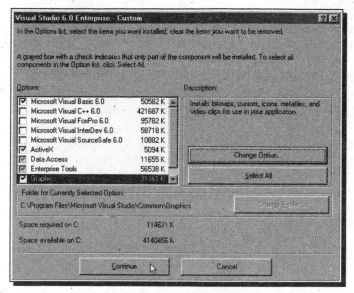

Fig. 1.3 Selecting Which Items to Install

As can be seen in Fig. 1.3, we opted not to install the other programming languages, just Visual Basic 6.0 and the other 'common' components. At any time in the future you can add or remove components to your PC from this box by re-running the Setup procedure.

When you click the **Continue** button the file transfer process begins, as long as you have enough hard disc space. When this is complete, click to **Restart Windows** if you are asked to.


## Installing the MSDN Help System

Microsoft, in their wisdom, no longer include any Help information actually built into the Visual Basic program. What they do provide is an MSDN library on separate CD-ROMs. This stands for Microsoft Developers Network and includes all the Help files and program samples that you will need. Once installed, this works fairly seamlessly with Visual Basic, but you have to install it yourself.

When your PC starts up again the Installation Wizard should be reloaded and should offer you the option to install the MSDN Library. If this does not happen, you should re-start the Setup program from the original CD and choose **MSDN** from the **Add/Remove** options. When requested, put the 'MSDN Library Disc 1 - Setup' into your CD-ROM drive. We suggest you then select the **Custom** option, as shown in Fig. 1.4.

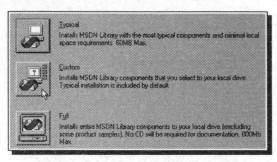

Fig. 1.4 The MSDN Installation Options

Selecting the options shown in Fig. 1.5 will let you use the complete Visual Basic documentation from your hard disc.

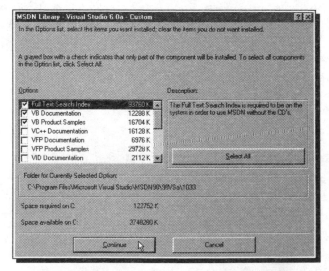

Fig. 1.5 Selecting the Visual Basic Documentation

When you click the **Continue** button the selected data files are copied to your hard disc, and you are given a chance to read about how to update your copy of MSDN on the Internet.

After a change of CD you should get a message box saying the MSDN installation is complete. There is probably only one more thing to do now.

## Installing the Service Pack

If your program package contains a Service Pack CD, this will contain 'enhancements and fixes' not included on the main program CDs. It is important that you install such a Service Pack. The CD in our package was called Visual Studio 6.0 SP3, but yours may be different.

When the CD is placed in the drive, the installation should automatically start, if not, use a My Computer window to look in its root folder and run the '.exe' file there. In our case this was *autorun.exe*. The actual installation was started, though, by the *SetupSp3.exe* file, which was located in the *enu* (English user?) sub-folder.

The last time we checked Microsoft's Web site, there was a Service Pack 4 available as a download for Visual Studio. If you have a fast Internet connection you could find this at:

    http://www.msdn.microsoft.com/vstudio

but be warned the total file size was 58 MB!

That should complete the procedure and you should now have a fully functional version of Visual Basic ready to go. We must admit that this was the most convoluted installation we have ever had to carry out, which is why we have spent several pages describing it.

# Some Housekeeping

Before getting too involved with Visual Basic we suggest you find where the Visual Basic files have been installed on your PC and carry out a couple of 'housekeeping' tasks.

## Visual Basic Folder Structure

When our version of the program was installed, the program files were placed in the VB98 folder on our hard disc, as shown in Fig. 1.6 below.

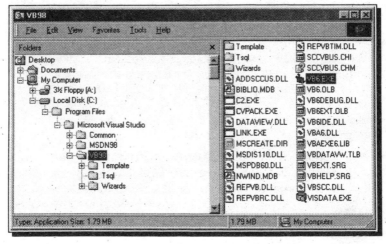

Fig. 1.6 Visual Basic Program Files and Location

This is a Windows Explorer view with the folder 'tree' structure in the left pane edited to simplify the path. Your folder structure may not be exactly the same, but you should not have too much trouble identifying it.

The important file here is *VB6.EXE*. This is the one that opens the Visual Basic program when it is executed. You could, if you were a masochist, double-click on this filename in the VB98 folder every time you wanted to start the program. There are obviously easier ways though. The Windows **Start** cascade menu is one, but using a Desktop icon is much easier.

## A Desktop Shortcut

Many programs these days automatically put a shortcut icon on the Windows Desktop as part of the installation procedure. Visual Basic does not do this, but it is very easy to do it yourself, once you have found the '.exe' file that opens the program.

To do this, simply open the VB98 folder in a My Computer window, select the file *VB6.EXE* and drag it, with the right mouse button depressed, onto your Desktop. When you release the mouse button a menu is opened as shown in Fig. 1.7, waiting for instructions.

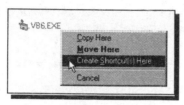

Fig. 1.7 Creating a Shortcut

Selecting the option **Create Shortcut(s) Here** and then editing the highlighted title below will give you the shortcut shown here to the left. Now all you have to do is double-click this icon on your desktop to start Visual Basic.

## A Working Folder

A folder missing from the list shown in Fig. 1.6, is one suitable for storing the programs (called **Projects** in Visual Basic speak) that you will be developing yourself. This is easily rectified, with the VB98 folder open in a My Computer window, right-click the mouse in the file area, select **New, Folder** from the opened menu, and name it Projects.

The reason for making the new projects folder a sub-folder of VB98 will become obvious in the next chapter, but if you prefer, you can place it anywhere on your system!

## Sample Projects

When you installed the MSDN Library on your PC you also installed a very extensive collection of Visual Basic sample projects. When you need inspiration it is well worth looking through these for programming ideas. We shall also be referring to them throughout the rest of the book.

Our installation placed these projects in the

```
C:\Program Files\Microsoft Visual Studio\
MSDN98\98VSa\1033\SAMPLES\VB98
```

folder, with each project having its own folder.

If you ever want more samples of Visual Basic projects and examples of coding, the best place to look first is on Microsoft's Web site at:

```
http://www.msdn.microsoft.com/vstudio
```

Look for the 'Samples and Downloads' section and obviously choose Visual Basic.

There are also literally thousands of other Web sites that cover the subject, but we will leave that for you to investigate.

Well that's enough to start with, in the next chapter we will introduce the programming environment that you will soon, hopefully, grow to know and love.

# 2

# The Visual Basic Environment

## Starting Visual Basic

 There are three main ways of starting Visual Basic. The easiest, as we saw in the last chapter, is to double-click a shortcut on the Windows desktop, like ours shown here. If you haven't made one yet, perhaps now is a good time!

The other way Microsoft provide you with is a little more of a fiddle and involves clicking the Windows Taskbar **Start** button, selecting the **Programs** option and finding **Microsoft Visual basic 6.0** (or whatever version you have) in the cascade menu system, as shown in Fig. 2.1.

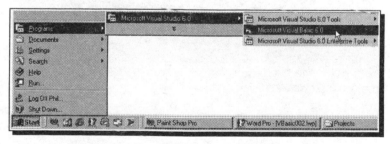

Fig. 2.1 The Start Cascade Menu System

You can also double-click on a Visual Basic project file (one with the extension .VBP or .MAK) in a My Computer window, in which case the project will be loaded into Visual Basic at the same time as it is started.

# General Windows Skills

We have assumed for the remainder of this book that anybody setting out to learn to program in the Windows environment will already be familiar with the workings of the Windows Graphic User Interface (GUI). We do not cover the basics of moving, re-sizing, iconising or generally manipulating windows, of handling the mouse, or menu systems. If you need more information on these skills, we suggest you first work through one of the books on Windows listed at the front of this book.

# The New Project Box

The first time you open Visual Basic the New Project dialogue box, shown in Fig. 2.2, appears. This can look daunting to a new user, but please don't panic. Most of the options are outside the scope of this book, and depending on your version of VB, may not be shown anyway.

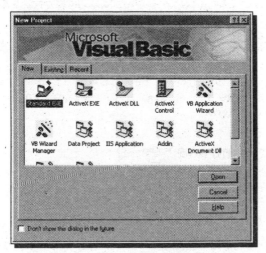

Fig. 2.2 The Initial New Project Dialogue Box

At this stage, make sure the 'Standard EXE' option is selected and click the **Open** button. If you want to find out more about this box you could click the **Help** button.

# The Visual Basic Window

The opening window of Visual Basic 6.0 is shown in Fig. 2.3, with some of the components slightly rearranged for clarity.

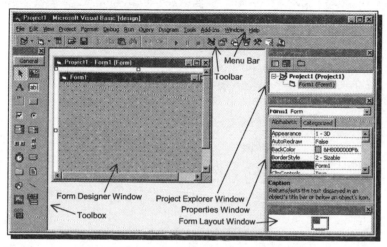

Fig. 2.3 The Visual Basic Working Components

When the program first starts, it is in 'design mode', as shown on the title bar above, with six separate elements making up the window. To understand the workings of the program we must spend some time looking at the various components that make up this window.

## Title Bar, Menu and Toolbar

This screen element contains the Title bar which shows the current project title, the operating mode and the normal windows control buttons, the Visual Basic menu bar, as well as the standard Toolbar below.

Fig. 2.4 The Visual Basic Title, Menu and Toolbar

By default, the Standard toolbar is displayed when you start Visual Basic. Other toolbars for editing, form design, and debugging can be toggled on or off from the **View**, **Toolbars** sub-menu. Toolbars can be docked beneath the menu bar or can 'float' if you select the vertical bar on the left edge and drag it away from the menu bar.

The standard Toolbar contains 21 buttons, or icons, to give shortcut access to some of the most commonly used menu commands. These are shown below, and will be detailed later as they become relevant to our text. Probably the icons you will use most are the Run and Stop controls.

The meanings of the Toolbar options are as follows:

| *Option* | *Action* |
|---|---|
| | Adds a project to the current project |
| | Adds a new form to the current project |
| | Opens the menu editor |
| | Opens an existing project |
| | Saves the current project |
| | Cuts the current selection to the clipboard |
| | Copies the current selection to the clipboard |
| | Pastes from the clipboard |
| | Opens the Find and Replace dialogue box |
| | Undoes last action |
| | Redoes last 'undone' action |
| | Starts to RUN the current project |
| | Stops execution and switches to break mode |

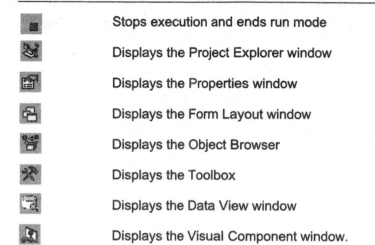

Stops execution and ends run mode

Displays the Project Explorer window

Displays the Properties window

Displays the Form Layout window

Displays the Object Browser

Displays the Toolbox

Displays the Data View window

Displays the Visual Component window.

## The Form Designer

In Visual Basic a form is the interface with the application you create. You can have multiple forms and place controls, text boxes and pictures on them when in design mode.

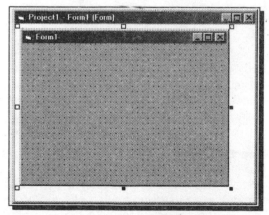

Fig. 2.5 The Form Designer Window

What you place on a form is what will be seen in a window when the application is run. To help when placing features on a form, by default, a grid is active, as shown in Fig. 2.5.

When new features are added to the form they automatically align themselves to the nearest grid positions.

## The Toolbox

This provides a set of tools that you use at design time to place different types of control objects onto a form. As well as the default toolbox layout, shown in Fig. 2.6, you can also create your own custom control layouts by right-clicking in the toolbox, selecting **Add Tab** from the context menu and adding the extra controls you want to the resulting tabbed section.

Fig. 2.6 The Toolbox

The standard Toolbox contains Visual Basic's intrinsic controls, which are outlined on the next page. These controls are contained inside the Visual Basic .EXE file. Intrinsic controls are always included in the toolbox, unlike ActiveX controls, which can be removed from or added to the Toolbox.

ActiveX controls, called custom or OLE controls in early versions of Visual Basic, are extensions to the Toolbox and exist as separate files with an .OCX file name extension. These include controls that are available in all editions of Visual Basic (such as DataCombo and DataList) and those that are available only in the Professional and Enterprise editions (such as Listview, Toolbar, Animation, and Tabbed Dialog). Hundreds of third-party ActiveX controls are also available to provide new 'functionality' for your applications.

The following table summarises the intrinsic controls found in the Visual Basic toolbox.

**Control Name** **Description**

**Picture box** - Displays bitmaps, icons, or Windows metafiles, JPEG, or GIF files. It also displays text or acts as a visual container for other controls.

**Label** - Displays text a user cannot interact with, or modify.

**Text box** - Provides an area to enter or display text.

**Frame** - Provides a visual and functional container for controls.

**Command button** - Carries out a command or action when clicked.

**Check box** - Displays a True/False or Yes/No option. You can check any number of check boxes on a form at one time.

**Option button** - With other option buttons it displays multiple choices as part of an option group, from which a user can choose only one.

**Combo box** - Combines a text box with a list box. Allows a user to type in a selection or select an item from a drop-down list.

**List box** - Displays a list of items that a user can choose from.

**Horizontal scroll bar** - Adds a horizontal scroll bar.

**Vertical scroll bar** - Adds a vertical scroll bar.

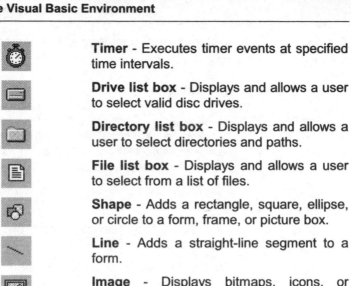

**Timer** - Executes timer events at specified time intervals.

**Drive list box** - Displays and allows a user to select valid disc drives.

**Directory list box** - Displays and allows a user to select directories and paths.

**File list box** - Displays and allows a user to select from a list of files.

**Shape** - Adds a rectangle, square, ellipse, or circle to a form, frame, or picture box.

**Line** - Adds a straight-line segment to a form.

**Image** - Displays bitmaps, icons, or Windows metafiles, JPEG, or GIF files; acts like a command button when clicked.

**Data** - Enables you to connect to an existing database and display information from it on your forms.

**OLE container** - Embeds data into a Visual Basic application.

The pointer tool is not a control. You click on it to return the pointer to its normal mode, when you want to move and re-size forms and controls.

## Project Explorer Window

In Visual Basic you can only have one project open at a time. The Project window displays a list of all the forms, modules, custom controls and all of the items contained in an open project. From the Project Explorer you can open the Form window for an existing form by selecting its name and clicking the **View Object** button. Similarly, you can open the Code window for an existing form by selecting its name and clicking the **View Code** button.

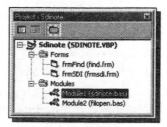

Fig. 2.7 The Project Explorer Window

The following lists all the project items that will be shown in the Project Explorer.

| | |
|---|---|
| Forms | All .frm files associated with the project. |
| Modules | All .bas modules for the project. |
| Class Modules | All .cls files for the project. |
| User Controls | All user controls for the project. |
| User Documents | All document objects, .dob files, in the project. |
| Property Pages | All property pages, .pag files, in the project. |
| ActiveX Designers | All designers, .dsr files, in the project. |
| Related Documents | Lists all documents to which you want a pointer. The path to the document is stored rather than the document itself. |
| Resources | Lists all of the resources you have in your project. |

If this window isn't open at any time, you can click its Toolbar icon, shown here, use the **View**, **Project Explorer** menu command, or use the <Ctrl+R> keyboard shortcut.

The Project Explorer is the quick way to access any of the components of a project in design mode.

## Properties Window

All the objects you create in Visual Basic (forms, boxes, command buttons, etc.), have a very detailed set of 'properties' which are controlled from the Properties Window, as shown in Fig. 2.8 below.

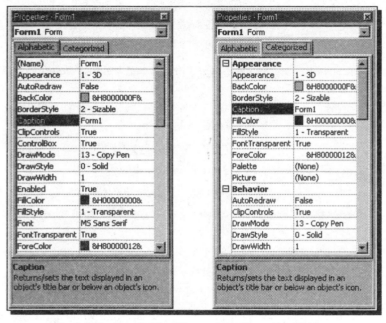

Fig. 2.8 The Two Tabbed Views of the Properties Window

 If it is not open, click the Properties Window icon on the toolbar, use the **View**, **Properties Window** menu command, or press the **F4** key.

The **Object Box**, at the top of this window, displays the name of the object whose properties are listed. Clicking its drop-down arrow (on the right) lets you select other objects from a list.

The two tabs, immediately below this, let you display the items in the Properties List, either alphabetically or in category groups, as shown in our examples in Fig. 2.8. These make it very much easier to find your way through the list.

The **Properties List** takes up the bulk of this window. All the properties available for the selected object are listed, with the current setting shown alongside. When you select a property name in the list a short description of it is given in the bottom of the window.

You change a property by selecting it in the list, and then either typing a new value in the property value box alongside it, or making a selection from the drop-down list of those available, as shown in Fig. 2.9.

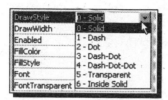

Fig. 2.9 Selecting a Property Option

The drop-down button 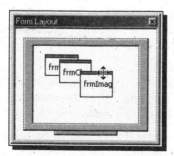, that you click to do this, does not actually show until you click the mouse pointer into the property value box.

## Form Layout Window

The Form Layout window, shown in Fig. 2.10, allows you to graphically position where your application windows will be placed on the screen at run time by dragging images around a simulated screen.

Fig. 2.10 The Form Layout Window

## Code Editor Window

This is the editor for entering application code. A separate code editor window can be created for each form or code module in your application, which makes it easy to cut and paste between them.

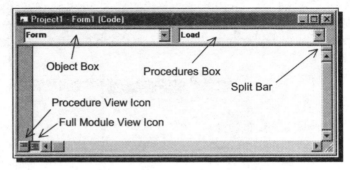

Fig. 2.11 An Empty Code Editor Window

The window components as shown in Fig. 2.11 are:

**Object Box** - Displays the name of the selected object. Clicking the arrow to the right of the list box will display a list of all the objects associated with the form.

**Procedures Box** - This lists all the procedures, or events, recognised by Visual Basic for the form or control displayed in the Object Box. When you select an event, the event procedure associated with that event name is displayed in the Code window below. All the procedures in a module are displayed in a single, scrollable, alphabetically sorted list. When you select a procedure from the two drop-down list boxes at the top of the Code Editor window the cursor is placed at the first line of code in the procedure.

**Split Bar** - Dragging this bar down, splits the Code window into two horizontal panes, each of which scrolls separately. You can then view different parts of your code at the same time.

**Procedure View Icon** - This displays the selected procedure only in the Code window.

**Full Module View Icon** - This displays the entire code in the module.

# Customising the Environment

## Dockable Windows

All the windows except the Form Designer have a 'dockable' property. A dockable window attaches itself to the nearest edge of the screen, or to the nearest other dockable window. When you move a dockable window around the screen, a rectangular box is displayed while the left mouse button is depressed, as shown in Fig. 2.12.

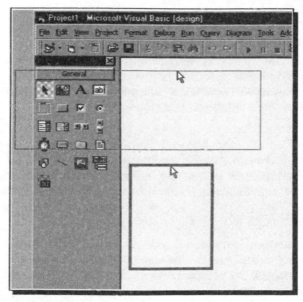

Fig. 2.12 Dragging Dockable Windows around the Screen

When you drag this box into the centre of the working window its lines become thick as shown in the lower box of Fig. 2.12. When the button is released the dragged window becomes an undocked or, 'floating', window. When you drag the box over a screen edge, as with the upper box above, it changes to fine lines and when released it 'snaps' to that screen location.

A docked window is dominant. If you drag the Toolbox, for example, to the top of the screen it docks there and all the other windows change size to accommodate it.

You can view the Dockable property of a window by right-clicking your mouse inside the window. If the word **Dockable** is checked, as shown here, the window is dockable. When a window is not docked, it is a 'floating' window. Windows that have their Dockable property enabled also have another property. They are 'always on top'. When they are open, they are visible and not hidden behind another window.

## The Working Environment

You don't really need all of these windows open all the time, and the screen is awfully cluttered, unless you are lucky enough to have a 19 inch monitor. It makes sense, then, to close at least some of the windows and perhaps to undock others. You have probably noticed by now that Visual Basic opens up every time with the screen arrangement and settings that were active when you last closed it.

The Project Explorer is an essential window. As your project grows, you will need it to get from one part of the project to another. But while you are designing your project's forms it will almost certainly be in the way. Click on the ✖ Close button in the upper-right corner of the Project Explorer to close this window. You can get it back when you need it by clicking the Project Explorer icon on the toolbar.

You use the Form Layout window only once for each form in the project, if that. So use the window when you first add a form to your project, then close it and use the toolbar to open it when you need it again.

While you are designing the user interface of a form, you will almost certainly need both the Toolbox and the Properties window. Once you have placed all your controls, however, you may want to close them to give you more room on the screen.

At the end of the day of course, it is all a matter of taste; you will set your development environment up the way you like it. You can always change it.

## Customising the Toolbar

There may well be options that are not on the standard toolbar that you would like to have available at the click of a mouse. Fortunately, it is easy to customise a toolbar as we shall see next when we add an icon that opens the Code Editor.

To do this, right-click in the standard toolbar and select **Customize** from the pop-up menu that appears. This opens the Customize window shown in Fig. 2.13.

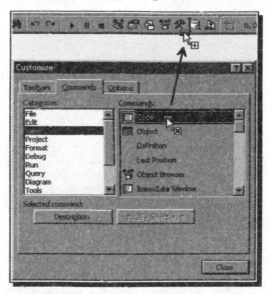

Fig. 2.13 The Toolbar Customize Dialogue Box

Select the **Commands** tab, click on **View** in the **Categories** list box and drag the icon for the Code Editor window to the main

Visual Basic toolbar, as shown in Figure 2.13. Drop it just to the right of the Toolbox icon. As we are sure you are aware, this is a 'drag and drop' operation and takes only seconds to carry out.

## The Options Dialogue Box

There are two general program settings that we think should be made before you start developing any projects. One change forces you to declare all your program variables, and the other offers to save your project before you attempt to run it. For both of these, use the **Tools**, **Options** menu command to open the Options dialogue box shown in Fig. 2.14.

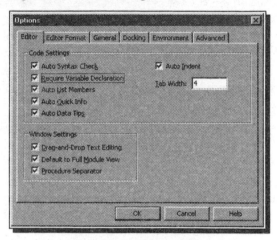

Fig. 2.14 The Options Dialogue Box

In this box you can change many of the Visual Basic program settings. On the **Editor** tabbed page, shown above, select the **Require Variable Declaration** option. Selecting this adds the 'Option Explicit' statement to general declarations in any new module, which means that you will have to explicitly declare, or define, all the variables you use in your projects. This can save a lot of problems when your code begins to get complex.

While you are in the Options box, make one more change. Select the **Environment** tab, click in the check box next to **Prompt To Save Changes**. With this checked, when you run a project from within Visual Basic, you are asked whether you want to save any changes you have made. Usually it is much safer to answer **Yes**, in case something goes wrong and you lose all your code. Have a look at the other options and then click the **OK** button to close the dialogue box.

# The MSDN Help System

As we saw in the first chapter, Visual Basic uses the powerful Help facility built into the MSDN library (Microsoft Developers Network) and provided on separate CD-ROMs. This includes all the Help files and program samples that you will need. When learning the program this is one of the essential tools to use. In fact, now Microsoft do not supply manuals, it is the only tool to use, without having to fork out more money to them. Hopefully you have installed MSDN? If not, read the first chapter and go back and do it straight away.

If all is well with the library, when you use the **Help**, **Contents** menu command from Visual Basic the MSDN window shown in Fig. 2.15 should open.

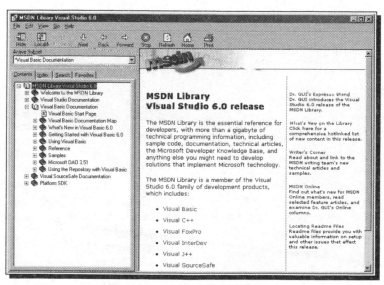

Fig. 2.15 The MSDN Opening Window

The format of this window should be familiar to anyone wanting to program in the Windows environment, but two points are worth special mention.

Firstly, depending on the installation options you used, you may need to have the MSDN CD-ROM in the drive to use Help.

Secondly, as MSDN includes documentation for all of Microsoft's vast range of development software, make sure you

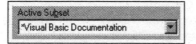

select the option **Visual Basic Documentation** as the **Active Subset**, as shown here.

There are two ways to access the general Visual Basic help. The first is to follow the links in the right-hand pane, until you get the information level you want. To get to the screen shown in Fig. 2.16, for example, we clicked the **Visual Basic** link, followed by that for **Programmer's Guide**.

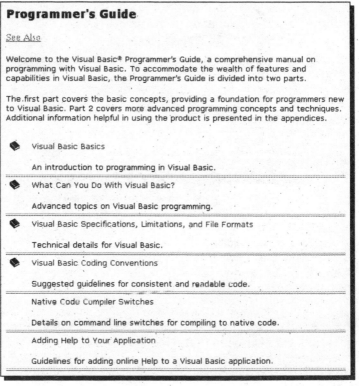

Fig. 2.16 MSDN Programmer's Help

You can then treat this like a book and read about any of the topics that interest you.

The second method is to use the tree structure in the **Contents** tabbed section, as shown in Fig. 2.17.

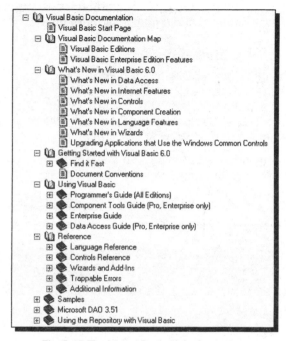

Fig. 2.17 The Visual Basic Help Contents

The **Contents** tab lets you scroll through a table of contents for Visual Basic Help. Clicking a '+' at the left of an item opens a sub-list, clicking a '-' will close it again. Clicking a list item, with the mark 📄 as shown above, opens its help text in the right-hand window pane.

The **Index** and **Search** tabs open up interactive Help index and search facilities. If the **Index** tab is clicked and you type the first few letters of a word in the input text box, you are shown the available options. Selecting one and clicking the **Display** button opens its page, but it may ask for the MSDN disc to be inserted.

The **Search** tab gives you access to a very powerful individual word search facility of the whole Help system.

The **Favorites** tab lets you keep a list of Help pages that you want to use again in the future. This is very useful, as the MSDN library contains an enormous amount of information and it is not always easy to find a particular page again.

## Context Sensitive Help

Once you have the MSDN library installed and working, it also provides the normal context sensitive help we are all used to with Windows applications. This is most useful to get help on the various Visual Basic windows and controls, as well as the programming language keywords and expressions.

To get help on something you have selected you simply press the **F1** key, to open a screen like that in Fig. 2.18.

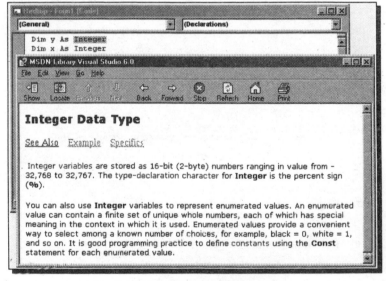

Fig. 2.18 Getting Context Sensitive Help

In most cases if you click the **Example** link you will be shown a code example using the keyword, etc., you want help on. In our case above, this is greyed out, so there was no example.

If you persevere with the Help system it will become an indispensable tool while you are using Visual Basic. However good you get, you will still need assistance on something!

# 3

# Programming Basics

## Programming Steps

With most programming languages you must write countless lines of code into an editor before anything happens. Some of this code might be written to control the operation of the program, but probably most of it will control the screen display and the interface with the final user of the program.

### Design Mode

With Visual Basic, on the other hand, you do not need to write code to set the program interface; you design this graphically on the screen in 'design mode'. All of the control features you are used to in Windows, such as menu bars, list boxes, control buttons, etc., can be almost instantly placed on 'Forms' at design time. When you are happy with the interface, you then enter code to control how its components interact with each other, and with the final user. Even this operation is made easy in Visual Basic, which names and controls your input procedures almost automatically.

### Run Mode

When you finally run the program, or project, that you have created, the Forms you designed become the program windows in 'run mode'. This means that Visual Basic gives you the power to use most of Windows' built-in facilities, like window manipulation, file opening and saving, etc., without having to write much program code at all. You can get really professional output with the minimum amount of effort, and that is always a good thing!

# A First Program

The next step forward has to be a simple programming example to show how these features fit together.

Start Visual Basic, or if it is already open, use the **File, New Project** menu command, and accept Standard.exe as the project type to create. If Form1 is not open on your screen, select it in the Project Explorer window and click the View Object button, also in that window. If the Properties window is not open, click the toolbar icon, shown here, or press the **F4** key.

## Creating an Object

Now, to start, we will add a button to the form. Click the Command Button icon in the Toolbox and move the pointer back over the form window. It should change to a cross hair. Position this cross at the place in the form where you want the top left corner of the button, hold down the left mouse button and 'drag' the button shape, as shown here. When you release the mouse button your new button will be placed on the form, with the name 'Command1' placed in it.

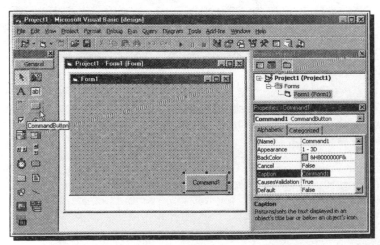

Fig. 3.1 Placing a Command Button on a Form

Another way of doing this, is to double-click the Command Button icon in the Toolbox, which places a new button in the centre of the form. You can then drag it to where you want it, then resize it.

During this operation you could have used the number indicators that appear when you are manipulating an object on a form. The Position Indicator, when you are dragging, shows the position of the top left corner of your button, while the Size Indicator, when you are re-sizing, gives its dimensions. By default, these dimensions are in 'twips', a standard unit of screen measurement equal to 1/20 of a printers point. In case you wanted to know, 1,440 twips equal one inch, and 567 twips equal one centimetre.

## Changing a Caption

The new button should be 'selected' in the form and have a series of black 'handles' around it, as shown in Fig. 3.1. If not, click it with the mouse. Now, look at the Properties window. The highlighted property in the list should be 'Caption', showing as 'Command1'. The caption is what actually appears on the face of the button.

Double-click the Command1 caption In the Properties window, to select it, and over-type it with the word **Print** instead. The button should now have a new caption on it. Changing an object's properties is as easy as that.

## Entering Code

Now double-click on the newly created button. This opens the Code Editor window, titled Project1 - Form1 (Code), with two lines of code and the cursor already placed for you. Type the following text:

```
Print "My first Windows 'program'?"
```

Your window should now look like that shown in Fig. 3.2. Don't worry too much about the rest of it at this stage, all will be revealed later.

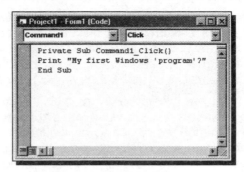

Fig. 3.2 Our First Code

## Running a Program

▶ For neatness, close the Code Editor window by clicking its ✖ Close button, and click the **Run** toolbar button, shown here, (or use **F5**, or the **Run**, **Start** menu command). Visual Basic changes to Run mode and displays the window Form1 containing our Print button. Clicking the mouse on this button prints the message in the window, as shown in Fig. 3.3.

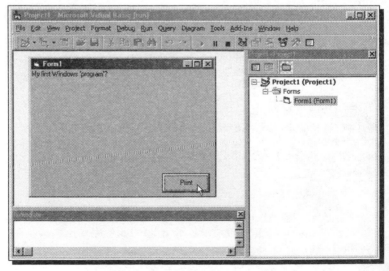

Fig. 3.3 Visual Basic in Run Mode

In Run mode all you can do at the moment is print the message every time the button is clicked. Not a very useful program, but it is a start. To stop the program running, and return to Design mode, click the **Stop** toolbar button, shown here. The easiest way to move between Run and Design modes is with the **Run** and **Stop** toolbar buttons.

## Saving a Program

We may use this example as the basis for other applications, so save it with the **File**, **Save Project** command, or the **Save Project** toolbar icon. Use 'EXAMPLE1' as the name for both the form and the project, when asked, as shown in Fig. 3.4.

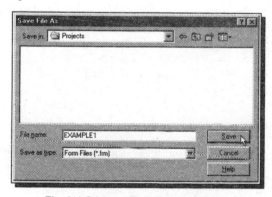

Fig. 3.4 Saving a Project and its Form

If you look in the Project Explorer window now, you will see the name changes have taken effect, as in Fig. 3.5 below.

Fig. 3.5 Project Explorer Window

# Project Elements

As can be seen from this very simple example, writing a program in Visual Basic follows a very definite series of steps.

- The interface is designed and built graphically, by placing controls and boxes, etc., on a series of forms.

- The properties of the forms, and controls used, are set to produce the visual results required.

- Code is written to link these up and generally make the program work. Essentially this code,

  - controls the general action of the program and,

  - determines how it will react when specific actions are carried out on specific objects by the end user, such as when a button is clicked, or a form double-clicked.

# The Interface

This consists of one, or more, forms with control features placed from the Toolbox, to enable the required program functions to be carried out by the final user.

## Forms

A form is a window, that opens at some stage when the program is run, and is used to either show information to, or get information from, the program user. When you start to build a new project Form1 is available to use straight away. If you need to open more, this is easily done with the Add New Form button on the toolbar. When saved to disc, every form in a project is saved in a separate file with a '.FRM' extension. This makes it possible to use a particular form in several different projects.

To include an existing form in an opened project, use the **Project**, **Add File** command. It will then be listed, and be accessible from the Project Explorer window. To remove one from an opened project, select it in the Project Explorer

window, click the right mouse button, and choose **Remove** ....
from the opened menu, as shown in Fig. 3.6.

Fig. 3.6 Removing a Form from a Project

Here, the form CALC.FRM has been added to our first example
project and is shown being removed as described above.

## Modules

Most of the code in a program, or project, will be included in the
various forms of the project. However the code attached to a
form is only usable by that form. For code to be available for
other forms, or the project as a whole, it must be placed in a
separate 'module'.

Code modules are stored with a '.BAS' file extension and are
very much like more traditional BASIC programs. They do not
have the power to get input from the user, or to create graphic
displays.

To open a module, use the **Project**, **New Module** menu
command, which opens the Add Module dialogue box shown in
Fig. 3.7 overleaf.

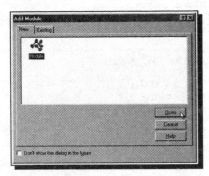

Fig. 3.7 The New Module Dialogue Box

A module can include:

- **Declarations** of constants, types, variables and DLL (dynamic-link library) procedures.

- **General Procedures** which can be called from anywhere in an application. These can be either **Sub** procedures, that do not return a value, or **Function** procedures, that do return one, or **Property** procedures.

## Applications

An application (or program), is a collection of forms and modules (as well as user controls and documents, property pages, ActiveX files and resources) that can be saved together as a project, and can be combined into a single executable file, with an '.EXE' extension. Forms and modules, and their code, can also be incorporated in other applications.

As you progress with Visual Basic you should build up a library of forms and procedures to use time and again. There is no point re-inventing the wheel every time you build a new application!

# Visual Basic Controls

As mentioned in the last chapter, controls are placed on forms from the Toolbox. The form below shows a composite of the more commonly used (intrinsic) controls and which icons are clicked on the Toolbox to produce them.

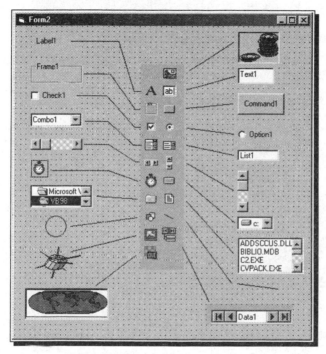

Fig. 3.8 Visual Basic's Intrinsic Controls

These controls should all be very familiar to any Windows program user. They form the building blocks to make up all types of dialogue boxes, etc.

We included some details of the individual Toolbox controls on Page 17, and most will be covered in more details as they are used throughout the rest of the book.

# Setting Properties

Once your forms and controls have been chosen and placed, their Properties have to be set in the Properties window, so that they look and behave in the way you want. Most of the default properties will not need to be altered; but some of the more important variables are now described.

## Some Form Properties

When designing a form you can set its position on the screen, and its size, graphically with the mouse. You can also set the

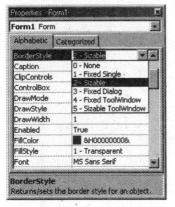

Fig. 3.9 Border Properties

*Left, Top, Width* and *Height* properties for more precise control.

The default form settings include a control box, minimise and maximise buttons on the title bar, and a re-sizeable frame. This lets the final user change the resultant window with these features, when the program is run. You can control all of these features though.

Setting the *ControlBox, Min-Button* and *MaxButton* properties to False will turn these features off when the program is run. Changing the settings to True will reactivate them.

The *BorderStyle* property works in conjunction with these in the following ways:

0 - None              Switches off all border or related border elements.

1 - Fixed Single      Can include Control-menu box, title bar, Maximise button, and Minimise button. The window is re-sizable only by using the Maximise and Minimise buttons.

| 2 - Sizable | The default setting. Re-sizable using any of the optional border elements. |
| 3 - Fixed Double | Can include Control-menu box and title bar; but not Maximise or Minimise buttons. It is not re-sizable. |
| 4 - Fixed Tool | Displays a non-sizable window with a Close button and title bar text in a reduced font size. |
| 5 - Sizable Tool | Displays a sizable window with a Close button and title bar text in a reduced font size. |

The best way to get used to all these settings is to change them, one by one, and then click between design and run modes from the Toolbar. For a very detailed description of a property and its available settings, simply highlight it in the Properties window and press the **F1** key.

*Caption* sets what text will display in the title bar, whereas *Name* controls the name of the form itself. Visual Basic needs every form in an application to have its own distinctive name. They are initially set at Form1, Form2, etc.

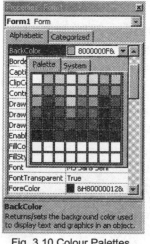

Fig. 3.10 Colour Palettes

*BackColor* sets the colour of the window, and *ForeColor* the colour of any text which is printed on it at run time. To change the colours simply double-click on the colour square to the right of the item in the property list and select from the palettes which open. The other attributes of such text can be controlled with the *Font* properties.

The *Icon* property lets you attach a different icon to your form window, which will replace the default Command Menu button and show in the Windows Taskbar when the window is minimised at run time.

You can select such icons from the extensive list of those provided with Visual Basic (in our case these were in the C:\Program Files\Microsoft Visual Studio\Common\Graphics\Icons folder), or you can design your own.

*MousePointer* determines the shape of the pointer when it is moved over the window at run time and *Picture* allows you to attach a graphic image 'permanently' to a window. Setting *FontTransparent* to 'True' will then let you print text on the graphic, without blocking it out.

## Label Properties

A label usually holds text on a form that is not changed interactively by the end user. The *Alignment* property determines whether the *Caption* text (limited to 1024 bytes) is Left, Right or Centre Justified.

When a label has its *AutoSize* property set to True, the *WordWrap* setting determines whether it expands vertically or horizontally to fit the text specified in its *Caption* property. With *WordWrap* set to True the text wraps and the label expands, or contracts, vertically to fit the text and the size of the font. The horizontal size does not change.

With the default *WordWrap* setting, False, the text does not wrap and the label expands, or contracts, horizontally to fit the length of the text and vertically to fit the size of the font and the number of lines.

To prevent a label changing size at all, leave *AutoSize* with its default setting of False.

## Text Box Properties

A Text Box is used to hold text, entered at design time, entered interactively by the user, or assigned in code at run time.

The *Text* property contains the text string that is displayed and *MaxLength* determines whether there is a limit to the length of the *Text*. The default is 0, or no maximum. Any number larger than 0 indicates the maximum number of characters that can be entered into the Text Box, (up to a maximum of 64K).

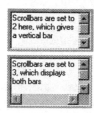

When *MultiLine* is set to True, the *Alignment* property forces left, right or centre alignment of *Text*. *ScrollBars* sets scroll bars as follows. The default, 0, sets no bars, 1 sets a Horizontal bar, 2 a Vertical bar and 3 sets both bars, as shown here.

## Command Button Properties

Command buttons are placed on a form so that the end user of the program can select them to begin, interrupt, or end a process. When selected they appear to be depressed.

The *Caption* property determines the text displayed on a command button. Clicking a button always selects it, but there are two other ways that should be used. With the *Default* property set to True, pressing <Enter> will select it; and with the *Cancel* property set to True pressing <Esc> will select it. The former would be used to determine what command is actioned in a window when the <Enter> key is pressed, and the latter to control the <Esc> key, maybe for exiting the box, or the program.

## Check Box and Option Button Properties

Check boxes are used to allow the user to easily choose if something is true or false, (switched 'on' or 'off'), or to choose more than one option from a selection. Option Buttons are used in a group to display multiple choices from which the user can select only one. The properties of both are similar. The *Value* property controls what state the object is in. When set at 0, the default, it is unchecked, at 1 it is checked, and at 2 it is greyed out, or dimmed.

When the *Enabled* property is set to True, the control is able to respond to events, such as a click from the mouse pointer. When set at False it is inactive.

A frame control would usually be used for grouping option button, or check box controls.

## The Tab Order of Controls

When a Windows dialogue box is active only one control on it has the 'focus' at any one time. This is shown by either a dotted box, as shown here, or a highlight, on the control. You move the focus round the box with the <Tab> key. When the <Tab> key is used in this way the current control 'receives the focus'. When you design a form you should make sure the tab order of the controls on the form is correct.

Initially the order is set automatically and is the same as the order in which you placed the controls. This order is actually controlled by the *TabIndex* properties of the various controls on a form. The control which will receive the focus when a window is opened should have a *TabIndex* value of 0, followed by values of 1, 2, etc.

To prevent the focus being given to a control you can set its *TabStop* property to False. Although the control still holds its place in the tab order, determined by the *TabIndex* property, the focus will not be given to it.

## Shortcut Keys

There is yet another way to select some of the controls in a running window, that is by pressing an <Alt+letter key> combination from the keyboard. To do this you place an ampersand, the '&' character, in front of the selected letter in the *Caption* property. This underlines the next letter on the control face. In our example on the left, the *Caption* entered was 'Cli&ck me'.

Most of the properties described so far are set during the initial design process. Many of them, however, will also be changed while the program is being run. This is done, either interactively by the user, or under the control of code written into the program.

# Writing Code

Visual Basic is unlike all the other programming languages we were brought up with. Most of the hard work building interfaces, etc., is done almost automatically for you, once you know how to steer the process. Lines of code are required, however, to string all the building blocks together and actually produce useful results.

It is very much an **event-driven procedure** based language, with each independent procedure designed to carry out a specific task. An event being an action which is recognised by a form or control.

## Code Editor Windows

As was introduced in the last chapter, the operation of writing your code is carried out in a special Code Editor Window. There are two main ways of opening a Code Editor window in design mode. The easiest is to double-click on the form, or control, whose code you want to edit. You can also select the form or control (in other words make it active by clicking it), and press the View Code button in the Project Explorer window.

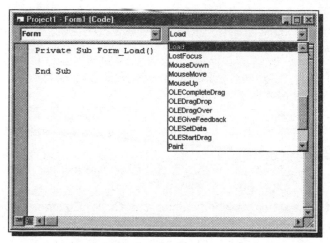

Fig. 3.11 Code Editor Window with Procedures Box Open

As described on Page 22, a Code Editor window contains two drop-down list boxes in its top bar. The **Object** box lists the current form and all the controls on it when you click its down button. The other, the **Procedures** box, lists all the events recognised by Visual Basic for the form or control displayed in the Object box.

Every form and control has a set of pre-defined events that it can recognise. The example on the previous page shows the events list opened for the empty form 'Form1'. The active event in the list is Load and the code in the form for that event is shown, ready to edit, in the lower half of the window. When you select an event, either the event procedure associated with that event name, or a code template for the event, is displayed in the bottom part of the Code Editor window.

Any code placed in this Load Procedure would be activated when the form was first opened. In this case, as the form is Form1 and would open first, the code would activate when the program is first run.

You write code to attach event procedures only for events to which you want a form or control to respond. If you leave an event procedure empty that event will produce no program action.

When writing code to attach an event procedure to a form or control you do the following:

1    Select the event in the Procedures box for which you want to add code.

2    Enter your code, in the template provided, in the standard way for entering code and declarations.

3    If necessary, select other forms or controls from the Object box in the Code Editor  window and follow the same process from step 1 above.

4    When finished, close the Code Editor window by double-clicking its control box.

Instead of using the template provided by Visual Basic, you can also create a new procedure by typing

```
Sub ProcedureName
```

in the Code Editor window. In the future, you can find this procedure by selecting (general) from the Object box and then looking in the Procedures box.

# Visual Basic Naming Convention

The standard syntax when writing an event procedure is made easier for you, as Visual Basic provides the names for procedures automatically. It combines the control name with the event name and separates them with an underscore character '_'. Thus the standard name is

```
Control_Event
```

In the open Code Editor window shown in Fig. 3.11, the procedure name shown was

```
Form_Load
```

This names the procedure that will activate whenever that form is loaded, or opened. This convention might seem a little confusing to start with, but it is so logical it soon becomes second nature.

The full syntax for an event procedure is:

```
Sub ControlName_EventName (arguments)

  Local variable and constant definitions
  Statements

End Sub
```

## Naming Control Properties

The control properties, described earlier in the chapter, are frequently assigned values or have their values changed, in program code. The usual format for this would be

```
ControlName.Property = expression
```

Where **ControlName** is the name of the control, **Property** is the Visual Basic name of the property concerned and **expression** is a valid expression (such as a text string, or arithmetic calculation). Note the '.' separating the property name. As an example, the code

```
Text1.Text = "Type a number here"
```

would place the text string 'Type a number here' into the *Text* property of the Text Box named 'Text1'. When this code is activated, that is the message that will show in that Text box on the form.

## Naming Controls

When you first create an object (a form or control), Visual Basic sets its Name property to a default value. For example, all command buttons have their Name property initially set to Command*n*, where *n* is 1, 2, 3, and so on. Visual Basic names the first command button drawn on a form Command1, the second Command2, and the third Command3, etc.

You may choose to keep the default name, as we do in many of our examples; however, when you have several controls of the same type, it makes sense to change their Name properties to something more descriptive. Because it may be difficult to distinguish the Command1 button on Form1 from the Command1 button on Form2, a naming convention can obviously help. This is especially true with complex projects, where an application may consist of several form, standard, and class modules.

You can use a prefix to describe the class, followed by a descriptive name for the control. Using this naming convention makes the code more self-descriptive and alphabetically groups similar objects in the Object list box of the Code Editor window. So they are much easier to find.

For example, you might name a Check Box control like this:

```
chkReadOnly
```

We have included recommended naming conventions in Appendix B. These are shown in more detail in the MSDN section on 'Visual Basic Coding Conventions'.

# 4

# Starting to Program

## Entering Program Code

With what was discussed previously in mind, activate Visual Basic and make sure the **Auto Syntax Check** option is selected in the **Editor** section of the Options box opened with the **Tools**, **Options**, command. This ensures that every entered line of code is checked for errors, with minor errors being corrected automatically. We will now create a program to calculate the average of three numbers, in order to demonstrate a few points.

Unlike QuickBasic, you can't just type code into the program and show the printed results straight on the screen when you run the code. The **Print** command does not print to the screen, but will print (after a fashion) to the background of a window. However, if there are any controls on the window, in the print area, they will block out the print output. A picture box receives print output better, but for the moment we will stick to using a plain window to demonstrate our code results.

Using the **File**, **Open Project** command, open the program EXAMPLE1, which should have been saved from Chapter 3. If not, take a few minutes and do the very basic example now. We will adapt Form1 as a work area for developing some programs to help come to terms with the basics of the programming language.

# Using the Code Editor

Double-click on the Print command button which should open the Code Editor window with the Command1_Click procedure showing. Delete the middle line of code, by selecting it and pressing the <Del> key, and type in the code shown in Fig. 4.1.

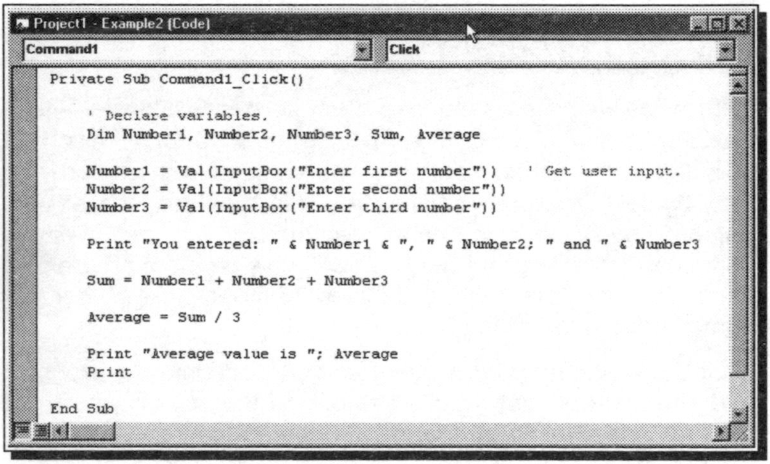
Project1 - Example2 (Code)
Command1
Click
Private Sub Command1_Click()
' Declare variables.
Dim Number1, Number2, Number3, Sum, Average
Number1 = Val(InputBox("Enter first number")) ' Get user input.
Number2 = Val(InputBox("Enter second number"))
Number3 = Val(InputBox("Enter third number"))
Print "You entered: " & Number1 & ", " & Number2; " and " & Number3
Sum = Number1 + Number2 + Number3
Average = Sum / 3
Print "Average value is "; Average
Print
End Sub

Fig. 4.1 The Code for Example2

This is presented to give you an idea of some Visual Basic source code. The statements in it will be discussed in more detail in the following pages, so there is no need to worry! But you will get some experience of the editor.

When you have entered a row of code, press the <Enter> key to start a new one. Note how the editor changes the entered code. It places spaces in the line, capitalises keywords, checks the line for syntax errors and changes the colour of some of the code. By default, Keywords are coloured blue and Comment text is coloured green in the Code Editor window. These colours make reading the code much easier.

If you attempt to leave a code line which contains an error, a message box, maybe similar to the one shown in Fig. 4.2, will open. Pressing the <Esc> key, or clicking the **OK** button, will remove the box. You can then correct the code straight away, or in the future. These messages can be a nuisance if you use the **Cut** and **Paste** facilities of the **Edit** menu. If so, you could turn off the **Auto Syntax Check** option described earlier, but we wouldn't recommend this.

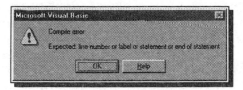

Fig. 4.2 Compile Error Message Box

## Automatic Code Completion

The Code Editor also makes writing code much easier with some special features that can help by completing your code statements, properties, and arguments for you. As you enter code, the editor displays lists of appropriate choices, statement or function prototypes, or values, depending on what you are doing.

When you enter the name of a control in your code, the **Auto List Members** feature presents a drop-down list of properties available for that control (see Fig. 4.6). If you type the first few letters of the property name it will be selected from the list and then just pressing the <Tab> (or <Enter>) key will complete its entry for you. This option is also helpful when you aren't sure which properties are available for a given control.

**Auto Quick Info** displays the syntax for statements and functions, as shown in Fig. 4.3. When you enter the name of a valid Visual Basic statement or function the syntax is shown immediately below the current line, with the first argument in bold. After you enter the first argument value, the second argument appears in bold, etc.

```
MsgBox |
  MsgBox(Prompt, [Buttons As VbMsgBoxStyle = vbOKOnly], [Title], [HelpFile], [Context]) As VbMsgBoxResult
```

Fig. 4.3 An Example of the Auto Quick Info Display

If you prefer, you can switch both these features off (and on again) in the Editor tab page of the Options dialogue box, opened with the **Tools**, **Options** menu command. You can then access the Auto List Members feature with the <Ctrl+J> key combination, and  the Auto Quick Info feature with the <Ctrl+I> key combination.

## Other Keyboard Shortcuts

To help you move around and get the best out of the program you can also use the following shortcut keys to access commands in the Code Editor window.

| *Shortcut Keys* | *Description* |
| --- | --- |
| F7 | View Code window |
| F2 | View Object Browser |
| Ctrl+F | Find |
| Ctrl+H | Replace |
| Shift+F4 | Find Next |
| Shift+F3 | Find Previous |
| Ctrl+Down Arrow | Next procedure |
| Ctrl+Up Arrow | Previous procedure |
| Shift+F2 | View definition |
| Ctrl+Page Down | Shift one screen down |
| Ctrl+Page Up | Shift one screen up |
| Ctrl+Shift+F2 | Go to last position |
| Ctrl+Home | Beginning of module |
| Ctrl+End | End of module |
| Ctrl+Right Arrow | Move one word to right |
| Ctrl+Left Arrow | Move one word to left |
| End | Move to end of line |
| Home | Move to beginning of line |
| Ctrl+Z | Undo |
| Ctrl+Y | Delete current line |
| Ctrl+Delete | Delete to end of word |
| Tab | Indent |
| Shift+Tab | Reduce indent |
| Ctrl+Shift+F9 | Clear all breakpoints |
| Shift+F10 | View shortcut menu. |

Now back to our example. Before running your code, return to the design form, select the Print command button, press the <Ctrl+C> Copy keys, followed by the Paste keys, <Ctrl+V>. You could also use the **Edit** menu commands, but using the menu is nowhere near as fast. Answer **No** to the question about creating a control array, (we don't want to know about such things at this stage!) and drag the two buttons until the new one is placed below the other. Now change its *Caption* property to 'Quit'. At this stage, that should be no problem, otherwise read through the last two chapters again!

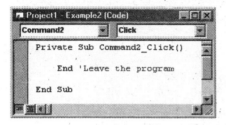

Fig. 4.4 The Quit Button Code

It is always a good idea to give the user of a program an easy way to leave it. Open the Code window for the Quit button and place the very lengthy code statement, shown in Fig. 4.4, in the Click procedure. The **End** keyword stops any more code being looked at by Visual Basic and hence ends the program.

To test the program out, click the Run toolbar Icon and your new window, with its two buttons, should open. Clicking the Quit button, should place you straight back to design mode. If not, check that the one word of code was entered properly!

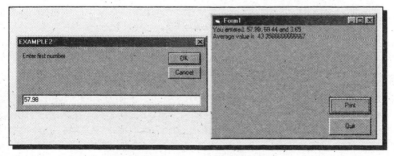

Fig. 4.5 Example 2 Output to Screen

Clicking the Print button, should open an Input Box, as shown on the left in Fig. 4.5, in which you enter data manually, in our case a number. Typing in a number and clicking the **OK** button will save the number as variable 'Number1' and open the Box again for 'Number2'.

When all three numbers are entered, the first Print command is actioned, the Sum and Average variables are calculated, and the final result is printed on the form, followed by a blank line (as shown on the right in Fig. 4.5).

All of which took many times longer to read, than to actually do!

## Program Comments

Our procedure code consists of statements and comments. Program Comments follow an apostrophe character ('), which can be placed anywhere on a line. Any text that follows this has no effect on the running of a program. This allows the insertion of remarks in the code to help the user remember the function of program sections. They also help the programmer in the future, we can assure you!

## Variables and Constants

### Variables

A variable is a quantity, or a string of text, that is referred to by name, such as Number1, Number2, Number3, Sum and Average in the previous program. Variables can take on many values during program execution, but you must make sure that they are given an initial value, as Visual Basic automatically zeros numerical variables, and 'empties' text ones, when a program starts.

# Constants

A constant is a quantity that either appears as a number (3 in the seventh executable statement in the previous program) or is referred to by name, but has only one value during program execution, allocated to it by the user.

# Expressions

An expression, when referred to in this text, implies a constant, a variable or a combination of either or both, separated by arithmetic operators.

# Naming Convention

Variable and constant names are formed by combining upper and lower case letters with numbers and the underscore character (_). Other characters and spaces are not valid and the first character must be a letter. The length of the name must not exceed 255 characters. When naming your variables, you should be careful not to use a name which is the same as a Visual Basic reserved word, otherwise you may get an error message.

To maintain compatibility with earlier versions of Basic you can add the following suffix type-declaration characters (%, &, !, #, @, and $) to variables to identify their type. A%, for example, would always be treated as an Integer by Visual Basic.

The very powerful *Variant* data type is the default for Visual Basic. This is the data type that is allocated to your variables if they are not explicitly declared as some other type. The Variant data type is a special data type that can contain numeric, string, date, or currency data as well as the special values Empty and Null.

There are a variety of other, more conventional, data types for both variables and constants; the most commonly used being the *Integer* and *Single* (single-precision floating-point) types. An integer type can hold only integer (or whole number) quantities and is distinguished from a floating-point type which holds numbers containing fractional parts. The computer stores these two types differently and tends to calculate much faster when using integer-value variables or constants.

Examples of integer and floating-point numbers are as follows:

| | |
|---|---|
| -255 | is an integer number |
| 26.75 | is a real, or floating point number |
| -.45E+16 | is an exponential number. The E stands for 'times ten to the power of'. |

Less commonly used types of numerical variables and constants are **Long** (long integers) and **Double** (double-precision floating point). In Visual Basic, the values of single-precision variables are accurate to 6 significant figures, while those of double-precision variables are accurate to 16. **String** variables can be as long as 65,500 characters.

As we saw above, you do not need to set the type of a variable, as by default, it will be a Variant and adapt to the data involved. There are many times, however, when you will find it necessary to force a specific data type in your code.

The following table shows the data types supported by Visual Basic, with their type-declaration suffix and the possible range of each data type.

| _Type_ | _Suffix_ | _Range_ |
|---|---|---|
| **Byte** | | 0 to 255 |
| **Boolean** | | True or False |
| **Integer** | % | -32,768 to 32,767 |
| **Long** | & | -2,147,483,648 to 2,147,483,647 |
| **Single** | ! | -3.402823E38 to -1.401298E-45 for -ve values; 1.401298E-45 to 3.402823E38 for +ve values. |
| **Double** | # | 1.79769313486232E308 to -4.94065645841247E-324 for -ve values; 4.94065645841247E-324 to 1.79769313486232E308 for +ve values. |
| **Currency** | @ | -922,337,203,685,477.5808 to 922,337,203,685,477.5807. |
| **Decimal** | | 28 decimal places with the smallest non-zero number being +/-0.0000000000000000000000000001. |
| **Date** | | January 1, 100 to December 31, 9999. |
| **Object** | | Any Visual Basic Object reference. |

| String | $ | Fixed length - 0 to approximately 65,400 characters. Variable length - Up to 2 billion characters. |
|--------|---|-----------------------------------------------------------------------------------------------------|
| Variant | None | Any numeric value up to the range of a Double or any character text. |

# String Variables

A sequence of characters is referred to as a literal, and a literal in quotation marks is called a string. For example, ABC123 is a literal, and "ABC123" is a string.

Like numbers, strings can be assigned to variables. They can be distinguished from numeric variables by a $ after the name, for example A$. A string can be assigned to a string variable with a statement such as

```
strAdd$ = "ABC123"
```

or with the more usual declaration and assignment

```
Dim strAdd As String
strAdd = "ABC123"
```

# Variable Type Declarations

As with QuickBASIC, variable types can be declared (at module level) with the use of the **Deftype** statement rather than using type declaration characters. This method however is really kept only to maintain compatibility. Using Dim type declaration statements is far easier.

The various Deftype declaration statements are as follows:

| *Deftype* | *Type of Variable* |
|-----------|--------------------|
| **DefBool** letter1 [-letter2] | Boolean |
| **DefByte** letter1 [-letter2] | Byte |
| **DefInt** letter1 [-letter2] | Integer |
| **DefLng** letter1 [-letter2] | Long |
| **DefSng** letter1 [-letter2] | Single |
| **DefDbl** letter1 [-letter2] | Double |
| **DefCur** letter1 [-letter2] | Currency |
| **DefDate** letter1 [-letter2] | Date |
| **DefStr** letter1 [-letter2] | String |
| **DefVar** letter1 [-letter2] | Variant. |

Named variables cannot be defined with the Def statement; what can be defined are all variables *starting* with the letter specified within the Def statement (as letter1 above). Ranges of variables can be entered with a hyphen in between their respective starting letters.

For example, to define all variables starting with letters within the range from I to N as integers, you could use

```
DefInt I-N
```

If a floating-point operand is assigned to an integer operand, the floating-point number is first rounded and then truncated to an integer, i.e., assuming that both I and K have been declared as integers (either by the statement **DefInt** I-K, or with **Dim..As**), the statements I=3.5 and K=0.37 will cause Visual Basic to assign the integer values of 4 and 0 to the constants I and K, respectively. For this precise reason, mixing floating-point constants or variables with integers in arithmetic operations, can have unexpected results! Thus, mixed mode arithmetic is best avoided.

## The Dim Statement

In Visual Basic this is the standard way to declare variables and allocate storage space to them. It was not strictly necessary in our program here (EXAMPLE2), but was used because it is considered good programming practice to declare and dimension any variables you use.

Dim on its own, as used in EXAMPLE2, simply declares what variables are used. They will be treated by the program as the Variant type.

To implicitly declare a variable's type the format is:

```
Dim Variable_Name As Type
```

where **Type** is one of those in the earlier list. Thus the statement

```
Dim intName As Integer
```

declares the variable 'intName' and ensures that it will always be considered as an integer.

It is usual to place **Dim** statements before any other code. When used in the Declarations section of a form or module, the variables declared with **Dim** are available to all procedures within the form or module. When used at the procedure level, as in our example in Fig. 4.6, the variables are available only in that procedure.

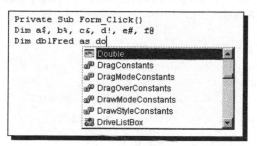

Fig. 4.6 The Auto List Members Feature

Here we were in the process of entering a Dim declaration into the Code Editor; as soon as we finished typing 'as', an Auto List Members menu opened, as shown, for us to select the type of variable we wanted. We carried on typing 'do' until **Double** was selected in the menu and pressed <Tab> to complete the declaration. The Editor then 'tidied up' the entry to the following:

```
Dim dblFred As Double
```

This example shows the two ways of declaring variable types. With type-declaration suffixes, as used in older versions of BASIC, and a full declaration statement using a 'long' variable name that is more descriptive. The first three letters of the name being standard, depending on the variable type. (See Appendix B for the conventional names used).

```
Private Sub Form_Click()
Dim a$, b%, c&, d!, ▊#, f@
Dim dblFred As Doubl Locale As Double
```

Fig. 4.7 Identifying a Variable Type

If you want to know a variable's type when using the Code Editor, highlight it, press the right mouse button and select **Quick Info** as shown above.

## The Val Function

This returns the numeric value of a string of characters. In our case, in EXAMPLE2, we did not prevent non numeric values being entered at run time. The Val function stops reading the string at the first character that it cannot recognise as part of a number. Val also strips blanks, tabs, and line feeds from an argument string.

## The InputBox Function

This function displays a prompt in a dialogue box, waits for the user to input text or choose a button, and returns the string contents of the text box. The syntax for the function is

```
InputBox(prompt [,title] [,default])
```

InputBox$ can also be used. In this statement:

**prompt**     is the required string expression displayed as the message in the box. If *prompt* consists of more than one line, you can separate the lines using a carriage return character (**Chr(**13**)**), or a linefeed character (**Chr(**10**)**), or both between each line. Make sure you put an ampersand character '&' before and after them though.

**title**     is the optional string expression displayed in the title bar of the dialogue box. If you omit the title, nothing is placed in the title bar.

**default**     is the optional string expression displayed in the text box as the default response if no other input is provided. If you omit *default*, the text box is displayed empty.

There are in fact three other optional arguments that can be used at the end of the above expression, before the final bracket ')':

```
[,xpos] [,ypos] [,helpfile, context]
```

With these you can exactly position the Input Box on the screen and specify a help file that can be opened.

If you click the **OK** button or press <Enter>, the **InputBox** function returns whatever is in the text box. Clicking the Cancel button returns a null string ("").

The **InputBox** statements provide one way of giving the variables in our example a value. The values for the variables Number1, Number2 and Number3 are entered directly from the keyboard. Once variables have values, they can be used in assignment statements and/or expressions in the rest of the program to perform desired calculations. A variable must have a value before it is used in an expression or in the right-hand side of an assignment statement.

## The Print Statements

The **Print** statements allow the printing of the result of our calculation. This result is held in the variable named Average. A string within full quotes following the **Print** command allows us to explain what is printed out. The statement **Print**, with no destination given, causes output to be sent to the current window. Note the use of the ampersand character '&' to concatenate strings and variables in one of the print statements. The statement **Print** on its own on a line, causes the program to print an empty line. This is useful for splitting up print output.

We will delay discussion on formatting output until the next chapter. However, the penalty of this in our program, is that we have to accept the default Visual Basic form of printing without any control on the number of digits printed out. Sometimes this can look ugly, as we are sure you have found out by now.

# Arithmetic Operators & Priority

We shall now examine how the various arithmetic operations in this program are performed. The calculations in the program are performed by the statements

```
Sum = Number1 + Number2 + Number3
Average = Sum/3
```

Combining them into one line, we could also write

```
Average = (Number1 + Number2 + Number3)/3
```

but **Not**

```
Average = Number1 + Number2 + Number3/3
```

It is important that the numerator of this expression is in brackets. If it were not, Visual Basic would evaluate first Number3/3 and then add to it Number1+Number2, which would give the wrong result. This is due to an inbuilt system of priorities as shown in the table below:

## The Arithmetic Operators

| Symbol | Example | Priority | Function |
|--------|---------|----------|----------|
| ( ) | (A+B)/N | 1 | Parenthesised operation |
| ^ | A^N | 2 | Raise A to the Nth power |
| * | A*N | 3 | Multiplication |
| / | A/N | 3 | Division |
| + | A+N | 4 | Addition |
| – | A–N | 4 | Subtraction |

## Additional Operators

There are two other operators which are useful when performing integer division. These are \ and **Mod**. The \ operator gives the whole number part of the result of a division, while the **Mod** operator gives the remainder. We suggest that you test these in a window.

For example, the program statement

```
Print 10\3
```

gives the result 3, while the program statement

```
Print 10 Mod 3
```

gives the result 1.

It must be stressed, however, that the numbers on which integer division (\) and **Mod** operate (called the operands) are first rounded up or down and then converted to integers. Thus, the statements

```
Print 10.1\3.1
Print 10.1 Mod 3.1
```

will give the same result as before, namely 3 and 1, while

```
Print 10.9\3.9
Print 10.9 Mod 3.9
```

will give the result of 2 and 3, respectively.

Visual Basic evaluates expressions, in the order of priority indicated in the table on the previous page. Expressions in parentheses (brackets) are evaluated first; nested groups in brackets are evaluated beginning with the innermost grouping and working outwards.

Using brackets, the order of priority of execution, and therefore the final value of an expression, can be changed. If a line has an expression which contains several operators of equal priority, Visual Basic will evaluate them from left to right.

Let's examine how a complicated expression such as

$$Y = (A+B*X)^2/C-D*X^3$$

is evaluated. We assume that A, B, C, D and X have values.

First the bracketed portion of the expression will be evaluated. Within these brackets the multiplication has a higher priority and therefore it will be evaluated first. Then, A will be added to it, resulting in a numerical value to which we will assign the letter Z. Now the expression is reduced to the following:

$$Y=Z^2/C-D*X^3$$

The above has two exponential expressions, the leftmost of which is evaluated first. Writing $Z_1$ for the result of $Z^2$ and $X_1$ for the result of $X^3$, the expression is now reduced to

$$Y=Z_1/C-D*X_1$$

Again, since division and multiplication have the same priority, the leftmost expression is evaluated first. Finally, the result of the multiplication is taken away from the result of the division and assigned to Y.

Of course, all this procedure is carried out automatically by Visual Basic, but if you intend to use complicated mathematical expressions you need to be familiar with it.

## The Assignment Statement

What appear as equations above are, in fact, assignment statements and not algebraic identities. As long as the values of variables on the right of an equals sign are known, the calculated result will be assigned to the variable on the left of the equals sign.

As an example, consider the following lines:

```
K = 0
K = K + 1
Print K
```

where the second line would be meaningless had it been an algebraic expression. In computing terms the statement means 'take the present value in K, add one to it and store the result in K'. When this line is executed, the value of K (set in the first line) is zero and adding one to it results in a new value of K equal to one. On running this program, Visual Basic will print the result

```
1
```

in the current window.

# Saving a Project

You can save a program by selecting the **File**, **Save Project** option which will save the current project (.PRJ) and all forms and modules in it. If you have any new forms or modules, you'll be prompted to save them, one at a time. Visual Basic automatically adds the default file-name extension .PRJ for projects, .FRM for forms, and .BAS for modules.

Fig. 4.8 File Menu Options

In our case, you should use the **Save Project As** command, (as you probably used a previous file as a 'template' to build the example). Save the project as EXAMPLE2.PRJ, so that you can modify it in the future, **BUT** make sure you save the form as EXAMPLE2.FRM. If you don't rename your forms for each example, you will end up overwriting the previous form every time.

To prevent this happening it is a good idea to use a separate folder for each project, but with small programs like ours this can get somewhat cumbersome.

## Saving Files

When you want to save the active form, or module, to disc you use the **File**, **Save Form...**, or **Save Form... As**, commands in the same way. You might want to do this so that a form or module is available, under a new name, for a different project. As shown in Fig. 4.8, the menu options actually change depending on the feature that is active at the time.

## Adding and Removing Projects

The **Add Project** and **Remove Project** options, shown above, let you combine several projects and all their component files into one. This is where the Project Explorer window comes in very handy, as they are shown separately in it.

# 5

# Input and Output Controls

A program can be made to assign values to variables by either entering information on the keyboard, reading information included with the code, or reading information from data files. Output can be directed to a picture box, message box or window; sent to the printer; or written into a file. Reading input from a data file and writing output to a data file will be dealt with in a separate section.

## Text Box Input

Text boxes can be used on a form to enter data from the keyboard. We have already used the InputBox statement earlier on, but we will examine the other method now. This will be illustrated by writing a program to calculate and display 15% of any number input into a text box.

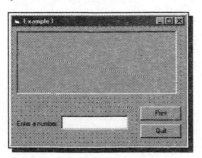

Fig. 5.1 Form Design for Example3

Open the previous program, EXAMPLE2.VBP and add a Picture Box, Label and Text Box, as shown in Fig. 5.1. We will use the Picture Box as a print area, the Text Box as an input area (so that the user can get information to the code), the Print button to start the calculation and print process and the Quit button to close the program.

When you are happy with the layout of the controls on the form, change the *Caption* and *(Name)* properties of the form to 'Example3', change the *Caption* property of Label1 to 'Enter a number:' and delete the *Text* property in Text1's property list, by selecting it and pressing the <Delete> key, to ensure that the box is empty when the program starts. While still in this list, set the *TabIndex* property to '0' (zero), to ensure that the focus is also in this empty box at start up.

As the Print button will control what action this program carries out we must write suitable code in its 'Click' procedure. Double-click the Print button, to open its Code window, delete the previous code between the Sub and End Sub statements and type in the following.

```
Private Sub Command1_Click()    ' Example3

Dim Percent As Integer    ' Dimension variables
Dim Number As Single
Dim Value As Single

Percent  = 15
Number = Val(Text1.Text)                ' Get number
Value = Number * Percent / 100

Picture1.Print Percent; "% of"; Number;
Picture1.Print "="; Value

Text1.Text  = ""              ' Empty the TextBox
Text1.SetFocus                ' Place focus in TextBox
End Sub
```

In the above, the keywords that are shown blue on the screen are highlighted, and comment text (green on screen) is in italics. You do not need to worry too much about spaces inside the statements, as the editor will sort these out for you. Leaving empty lines in the code does not affect the running of a program, but can make the code easier to read.

Save the program and form as EXAMPLE3, and then try running it. Every time you enter a number and press the Print button, a result line is printed in the Picture Box.

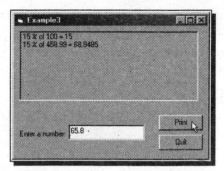

Fig. 5.2 The Window at Run Time

The code for Example3 declares three variables to be used in the routine, one as Integer type and the others as Single. If necessary, look back at the last chapter to see the difference. The 'Percent' variable is set as a constant with the statement

```
Percent  = 15
```

This is one way of giving a value to a variable, but the value cannot be changed, except by changing the statement in the code.

The next line

```
Number = Val(Text1.Text)
```

is much more flexible. The value placed in the variable 'Number' depends on the text in Text Box 'Text1' at the time the Print button was pressed.

The **Val** function is there to ensure that only numeric data is passed to the variable. If you try entering different combinations of numbers and letters, you will see very quickly how **Val** works. It accepts any numeric entry until a non-number character is entered and ignores anything else. If you enter '556PP89007', for example, only the number 556 will be passed.

## Changing a Property

The last two lines of code in EXAMPLE3.VBP change two of the properties of the Text Box, named Text1, when that section of the code is run.

At any one time the *Text* property of a Text Box determines what will be displayed in that box. In our program, once a number is entered, processed and printed, we do not want it to still display in the input box as it would interfere with future entries. The statement

```
Text1.Text  = ""
```

resets the *Text* property to contain whatever is held between the inverted commas. In other words, nothing. Note that ("") is, in Visual Basic, a string **not** a zero. If, as in our case, you want to use the box contents for numerical calculations, a 'Mixed Variables' error will be developed, unless you convert the string to a number with the **Val** function.

## Setting an Object's Focus

The user of our program can only enter numbers into Text1 when the Text Box 'has the focus'. The box is then active with the insertion point placed in it. Earlier on we set the *TabIndex* property to '0', to ensure that the focus is in the box at start up. This can also be done in code, as with the line

```
Text1.SetFocus
```

which places the focus in the empty Text Box, ready to receive new input from the keyboard.

# More on Print Output

In the last program, the lines of code

```
Picture1.Print Percent; "% of"; Number;
Picture1.Print "="; Value
```

control what is printed by our program and where it is placed. Picture1.**Print** will send print output to the Picture Box named Picture1 and start printing at the beginning of its top line.

**Print**, on its own, will send output to the current form itself, (the one holding the code), as shown here. This also shows that the print result flows behind any controls on the window; the Picture Box frame, in our example. Printed output to a form, or Picture Box, does not scroll when it reaches the end of the print area. Any further output is simply lost.

If variables within a Print statement are separated by semicolons, Visual Basic writes their value close together with no intervening space. If you leave spaces, when entering code, they will be replaced with semicolons when you move out of the line. A semicolon at the end of a line, as above, will force the next Print statement to continue on that line.

If variables within a Print statement are separated by commas the values of these variables are displayed on the same line, left-justified within inbuilt print zones. These print zones have an 'average' width depending on the font and size that is being used. As most fonts these days are proportional (the widths of characters displayed vary with their size) such output can be erratic, especially if you want neatly lined up columns!

If a string is included within a Print statement, such as "% of" in our example, on execution Visual Basic displays the actual characters within the quotation marks exactly as they appear in the statement. It is a way of providing captions or headings for the output.

## Formatting with Tabs

Presentation of tabular results can often be made easier to understand by using custom Tabs with the Print statement which allows output to be displayed in columns of your own design.

The program below illustrates this feature.

```
Private Sub Form_Click () ' Example4 - Using Print Tabs

Dim A, B, C
A = 15: B = 25: C = 10

    Print Tab(5); "A"; Tab(10); "B"; Tab(15); "C"
    Print Tab(4); A; Tab(9); B; Tab(14); C

End Sub
```

To enter it as EXAMPLE4.VBP, type the code as a Click procedure in the Form Code Window of a new file. When you run the program, click the window that opens, to activate the code. This simple method is useful for testing the code we present, as well as the numerous examples given in the Help section of Visual Basic. If you like, you can maximise the window to 'simulate' the older type Basic program environment.

When this program is run, Visual Basic will respond by writing the following to the window

```
A      B      C
15     25     10
```

Another useful formatting function is the **Print Spc** statement which provides a number of spaces between the last printed position and the next one. For example, the first Print line of the previous program could be replaced by

```
Print Spc(4); "A"; Spc(4); "B"; Spc(4); "C"
```

which would give a similar output if you were using a non proportional font, such as Courier New. To try this place the following two lines before the above Print statements. As you can see, it is quite easy to control the font style of the printed output.

```
Form1.FontName = "Courier New"
Form1.FontSize = 10
```

The **Print Tab** or **Print Spc** statements cannot be used to move to the left of a current printing position in a given line. Only progressive moves to the right are obeyed.

Note: Although tabulation using the **Tab** and **Spc** statements can work very well with whole numbers, using this method to format tables with floating-point numbers doesn't always work because of the number of significant digits.

## Print Locations

The Visual Basic co-ordinate properties *CurrentX* and *CurrentY* positions the 'print head' at any point on the object (e.g. Form or Picture Box), and printing starts at that location, irrespective of the print head's previous position.

*CurrentX* determine the horizontal and *CurrentY* the vertical co-ordinates for the next printing operation.

Co-ordinates are measured from the upper-left corner of a Form or Picture Box object, with *CurrentX* being 0 at an object's left edge and *CurrentY* 0 at its top edge. By default, co-ordinates are expressed in *twips*, or the current scale defined by the *ScaleHeight, ScaleWidth, ScaleLeft, ScaleTop,* and *ScaleMode* properties of the object being printed on.

The **Cls** (Clear Screen) command clears the current print object, (Form or Picture Box), and sends the print head to the upper left-hand corner of the object, position (0,0). You could place the command code

```
Picture1.Cls
```

in the Code Window of a command button. In which case clicking the button would clear the Picture Box Picture1, ready for new print output.

The next programs give examples of the co-ordinate system usage, the first prints an asterisk character (*) towards the middle of a window opened to full screen. Type the code as a Click procedure in the Form Code window of a new file

```
Private Sub Form_Click ()              ' Program EXAMPLE5
   Form1.FontName = "Courier New"   ' Set font style
      Form1.FontSize = 10

      Form1.CurrentX = 39  ' Position at window centre
      Form1.CurrentY = 14
   Form1.Print "*"             ' Print asterisk
End Sub
```

Then change the following properties for Form1.

| *Property* | *Setting* |
|------------|-----------|
| *ScaleMode* | 4 - Character |
| *WindowState* | 2 - Maximized |

*ScaleMode* determines the dimension units used in window settings and the above sets the dimensions as characters. With a maximised *WindowState* and the font style used, of 10 Point, Courier New, a window on one of our screens was 80 characters wide and 29 characters high. With higher resolution screen settings, these are obviously not the same.

The *CurrentX* and *CurrentY* properties in the following program place an asterisk at each corner of an 80 character wide x 29 high screen. Note that position (0,0) is the top left corner position, not (1,1), as we would have expected. So position 79 in used the X-direction, instead of position 80 when placing the asterisks at the right edge of the screen.

```
Private Sub Form_Click ()            ' Program EXAMPLE6
    Form1.FontName = "Courier New"       ' Set font
    Form1.FontSize = 10

  Form1.CurrentX = 0    ' Position top left
  Form1.CurrentY = 0
  Form1.Print "*"

  Form1.CurrentX = 79   ' Position top right
  Form1.CurrentY = 0
  Form1.Print "*"

  Form1.CurrentX = 0    ' Position bottom left
  Form1.CurrentY = 28
  Form1.Print "*"

  Form1.CurrentX = 79   ' Position bottom right
  Form1.CurrentY = 28
  Form1.Print "*"

End Sub
```

**Note:** This program has repeated statements and would obviously benefit from some of the techniques covered in the next Chapter.

# Formatting Functions

Up to now we have let Visual Basic display numbers with no regular structure, but just 'how they come'. This is sometimes satisfactory, but when not, the program has a very powerful formatting facility. The **Format** function converts any number to a **Variant** (and **Format$** to a string) with a specific number, date or time format according to the instructions contained in the 'format expression' shown below.

```
Format(variable, "format expression")
```

The easy way to format numbers is to use the following set of common format names that have been built into Visual Basic.

| *Format name* | *Description* |
|---|---|
| **General Number** | Displays the number as it is, with no thousand separators. |
| **Currency** | Displays the number with thousand separators and two digits to the right of the decimal point. Displays negative numbers in parentheses. |
| **Fixed** | Displays at least one digit to the left and two digits to the right of the decimal separator. |
| **Standard** | Displays numbers with thousand separators and two digits to the right of the decimal separator. |
| **Percent** | Displays numbers, multiplied by 100, with two digits to the right of the decimal separator and followed by a percent sign (%). |
| **Scientific** | Uses standard scientific notation. |
| **Yes/No** | Displays **No** if number is 0, otherwise displays **Yes**. |
| **True/False** | Displays **False** if number is 0, otherwise displays **True**. |
| **On/Off** | Displays **Off** if number is 0, otherwise displays **On**. |

You simply place the *Format name* in the above syntax expression, in inverted commas. You can also create your own formats with standard characters that are explained later.

As usual the best way to demonstrate something is to do it, so enter the program below into a new form.

```
Private Sub Form_Click ()              ' Program EXAMPLE7
                                 ' Use of number formats

Dim = Number
Number = 586786.980067453          ' Set initial value

Print "General format", Format (Number, "General Number")
Print "Currency format", Format (Number, "Currency")
Print "Fixed format", , Format (Number, "Fixed")
Print "Standard format", Format (Number, "Standard")
Print "Percent format", Format (Number, "Percent")
Print "Scientific format", Format (Number, "Scientific")
Print "Yes/No format", Format (Number, "Yes/No")
Print "True/False format", Format (Number, "True/False")
Print "On/Off format", , Format (Number, "On/Off")

End Sub
```

The result of running this code is shown in Fig. 5.3 below, which demonstrates the available formats quite well.

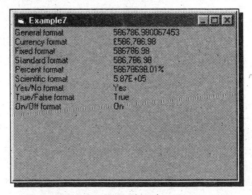

Fig. 5.3 The Visual Basic Common Formats

## User Defined Formats

As well as the common pre-defined format types, you can build your own using a series of 'special characters'. If you need to get this detailed, we suggest you spend some time coming to terms with Appendix C, which lists the available format characters, and the MSDN Help section on the Format function, as shown in Fig. 5.4.

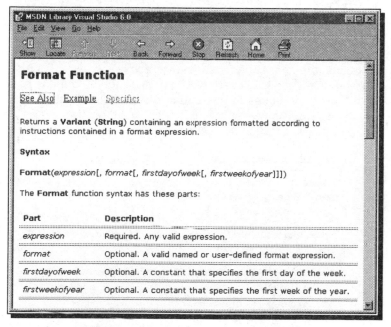

Fig. 5.4 Visual Basic Help on the Format Function

Clicking the Example link opens sample code on custom formats. Try out this example yourself, by highlighting the code, copying it to the clipboard, and then pasting it into the Declarations section (Click event) of a new form. You will need to add **Print** commands yourself though, otherwise nothing happens! Then press **F5** and click the form to run the code.

This is one of the very user friendly parts of the Visual Basic package. The Help facility provides example code to demonstrate most of Visual Basic's functions and features.

# Using Message Boxes

Another way of getting output to the screen is to use the message box statement, MsgBox. This can be used simplistically to display a short message on the screen. For example, the following code

```
Private Sub Form_Click()

MsgBox "A short message"

End Sub
```

produces the message box, shown above, when the object 'holding' this code is clicked. Not very exciting yet, but it is easy to get message boxes to give much more useful output. Below we have modified EXAMPLE2.VBP so that its output is displayed in a message box (see Fig. 5.5).

```
Private Sub Command1_Click()    ' Example7a

    ' Declare variables.
    Dim Number1, Number2, Number3, Sum, Average, NL
    Dim strMsg As String

    NL = Chr(10) 'Define NL as newline character

    ' Get user input.
    Number1 = Val(InputBox("Enter first number"))
    Number2 = Val(InputBox("Enter second number"))
    Number3 = Val(InputBox("Enter third number"))

    ' Build the message to be output
    strMsg = "You entered: " & Number1 & ", " & Number2
    strMsg = strMsg & " and " & Number3 & NL & NL

    Sum = Number1 + Number2 + Number3

    Average = Sum / 3

    strMsg = strMsg & "Average value is "
    strMsg = strMsg & Format(Average, "Fixed")

    MsgBox strMsg          'Send final output to Message Box

End Sub
```

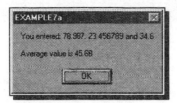

Fig. 5.5 More Complex Message Box Output

This works by building up the final message to be output in the string variable called strMsg. The various parts of the message are concatenated together using the ampersand '&' operator, as follows

```
strMsg = strMsg & "next part of message.."
```

Using the **CHR** function in the statement

```
NL = CHR(10)
```

returns the ANSI control character (10), the linefeed character. So whenever Chr(10) or, in our case NL, appears in the message string a newline is forced.

To format the result of the calculated output the expression

```
Format(Average, "Fixed")
```

is used. The **Format** function was covered several pages back, and in this case it converts the final number to "Fixed" format, with two decimal points.

You may have noticed by now that our EXAMPLE7a does not, in fact, need an open window to run. The input is obtained from Input boxes and the output is shown on a Message box. Thus the form and command buttons have become redundant.

To make this project run without the opening window, use the **Project**, **Add Module** command to add a new module, as shown in Fig. 5.6. Type

```
Sub Main
```

and press the <Enter> key. Visual Basic opens a Sub Procedure called **Main**. Copy the code from the previous example inside the main template, as shown in Fig. 5.6, and save the module as EXAMPLE7b.BAS.

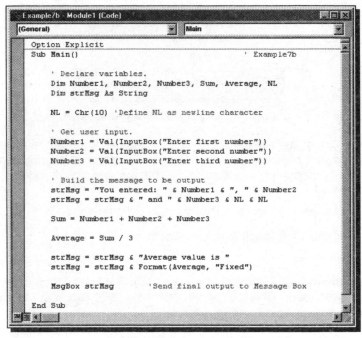

```
Example7b - Module1 (Code)

(General)                              ▼  Main                        ▼

    Option Explicit
    Sub Main()                                      ' Example7b

        ' Declare variables.
        Dim Number1, Number2, Number3, Sum, Average, NL
        Dim strMsg As String

        NL = Chr(10) 'Define NL as newline character

        ' Get user input.
        Number1 = Val(InputBox("Enter first number"))
        Number2 = Val(InputBox("Enter second number"))
        Number3 = Val(InputBox("Enter third number"))

        ' Build the message to be output
        strMsg = "You entered: " & Number1 & ", " & Number2
        strMsg = strMsg & " and " & Number3 & NL & NL

        Sum = Number1 + Number2 + Number3

        Average = Sum / 3

        strMsg = strMsg & "Average value is "
        strMsg = strMsg & Format(Average, "Fixed")

        MsgBox strMsg              'Send final output to Message Box

    End Sub
```

Fig. 5.6 A 'Self Starting' Module

When you run this project, the first Input box should open straight away. With Visual Basic, a project usually starts from Form1, (unless you specify another form), or from the Sub Main procedure of a module. If you get this wrong, an error message will open, with the following Help information.

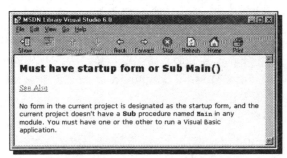

```
MSDN Library Visual Studio 6.0
File Edit View Go Help

Show    Locate  Previous Next   Back  Forward Stop  Refresh Home  Print

Must have startup form or Sub Main()

See Also

No form in the current project is designated as the startup form, and the
current project doesn't have a Sub procedure named Main in any
module. You must have one or the other to run a Visual Basic
application.
```

Fig. 5.7 Startup Error Help Message

To set the start-up object, open the Project Properties dialogue box shown in Fig. 5.8, with the **Project**, **Prop_erties** menu command.

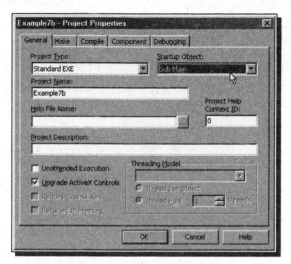

Fig. 5.8 The Project Properties Box

As shown above, our example has Sub Main set as its **Startup Object**. This dialogue box contains some pretty heavy features, way beyond the scope of this book. The **Help** button is well worth pressing. Note that it is here that you can give your project a unique **Project Name**, which is used internally by Windows. This is not the same as the file name, but appears on the title bar, as shown in Fig. 5.8.

We suggest you have a good look at the Project Properties dialogue box, some of its features will come into play when you come to make an executable .EXE file from your project code. Maybe not yet though, with the type of projects we are starting with!

## MsgBox Syntax

Visual Basic gives you easy access to some ten different types of message boxes, having different combinations of buttons and icons on them.

The full syntax for the MsgBox statement is

**MsgBox**(prompt[, buttons] [, title] [, helpfile, context])

The parameters must be used in the correct sequence and have the following meanings:

| *Parameter* | *Description* |
|---|---|
| prompt | The required string expression to be displayed as the message. The maximum length of prompt is approximately 1024 characters. |
| buttons | An optional numeric expression that specifies what buttons to display and the icon style to use. If omitted, the default value for buttons is 0. |
| title | The optional string expression displayed in the title bar of the message box. |
| helpfile | The optional string expression that identifies the context-sensitive Help file to be used. |
| context | The Help context number assigned to the appropriate Help topic by the author. |

If you want to omit any 'middle' parameters you need to show this by including their comma placeholders. To display a default message box, for example, with a specified title you should use the following format

```
MsgBox "Prompt", , "Title"
```

If you type the text strings straight into the statement you need to enclose them in inverted commas, as above. To include inverted commas themselves in the string you would have to enter two together for each one.

# MsgBox Buttons

The buttons argument settings are:

| Constant | Value | Buttons and/or Icons Displayed |
|---|---|---|
| vbOKOnly | 0 | OK button only. |
| vbOKCancel | 1 | OK and Cancel buttons. |
| vbAbortRetryIgnore | 2 | Abort, Retry, and Ignore buttons. |
| vbYesNoCancel | 3 | Yes, No, and Cancel buttons. |
| vbYesNo | 4 | Yes and No buttons. |
| vbRetryCancel | 5 | Retry and Cancel buttons. |
| vbCritical | 16 | Critical Message icon. |
| vbQuestion | 32 | Warning Query icon. |
| vbExclamation | 48 | Warning Message Icon. |
| vbInformation | 64 | Information Message icon. |

When entering a 'Buttons' parameter you can use the actual number values above, or preferably, the constants shown. These constants are specified by Visual Basic for Applications and can be used anywhere in your code in place of the actual

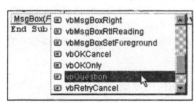

values. We strongly recommend you use the constants as their meaning is obvious wherever they are used, which cannot be said for the numbers themselves! They are also easily accessed from the Code Editor's **Auto List Members**

Fig. 5.9 Auto List Members

feature, shown here, that presents a drop-down list of available properties as you type in your MsgBox statement.

To help to visually show the differences between the different message boxes we show all the possible combinations of buttons and icons in the next three figures. Each one is named with its button constant.

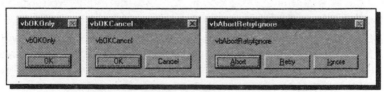

Fig. 5.10 Message Box Button Styles (0, 1 and 2)

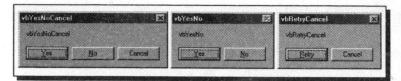

Fig. 5.11 Message Box Button Styles (3, 4 and 5)

Fig. 5.12 Message Box Button Styles (16, 32, 48 and 64)

## MsgBox Returned Values

When a message box is opened in a running program, Visual Basic waits for the user to click a button, and returns an Integer indicating which of the seven available buttons the user clicked.

The values returned are:

| Constant | Value | Button Pressed |
|----------|-------|----------------|
| vbOK | 1 | OK |
| vbCancel | 2 | Cancel |
| vbAbort | 3 | Abort |
| vbRetry | 4 | Retry |
| vbIgnore | 5 | Ignore |
| vbYes | 6 | Yes |
| vbNo | 7 | No |

These return values, or their constants, can be used in your code to determine what action to take, depending on which button was pressed.

# 6

# Control of Program Flow

## Control Structures

Visual Basic can force a section of code to be repeated by using the **For...Next** loop, in the same way as other standard Basics, or with the **While...Wend** loop, in the same way as other enhanced versions of Basic. In addition to these, Visual Basic upgrades the **While...Wend** loop with the **Do** loop, which tests for a condition either at the beginning or the end of the loop.

In standard Basic, decisions are made by using the **If...Then** statement, while in more advanced versions of Basic the **If...Then...Else**, **On...Goto**, and **On...Gosub** statements are also used. Visual Basic advances these with the addition of the block **If...Then...Else...Endif** and the **Select Case** statements.

## The For...Next Loop

The **For** and **Next** statements are used to mark the beginning and ending points of program loops. Any statements between the **For** and its corresponding **Next** will be executed repeatedly according to the conditions supplied by the 'control variable' within the **For** statement. An example is given below, and the code is shown in Fig. 6.1.

```
Private Sub Form_Click ()    ' EXAMPLE9

For K = 1 To 5 Step 1
    Print K
Next K

End Sub
```

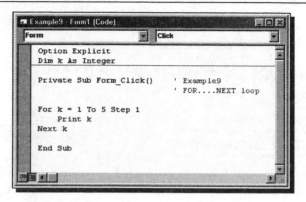

Fig. 6.1 A Simple Loop Counter

The above dimension statement was put in the **(General)** **(Declarations)** section, so that it could be available for all the project controls. The Code Editor window is shown in Full Module View (see page 22), so all the code is visible. In this view if you click inside a procedure's code, the Object and Procedures boxes (at the top) change contents, to indicate the event involved.

Within the **For** statement, the control variable k is assigned the value 1 which is increased repeatedly by the number following **Step** until it reaches 5. It thus has the values 1, 2, 3, 4 and 5. Since it cannot have these values simultaneously, a loop is formed beginning with the **For** and ending with the **Next**. The statements within the loop are executed five times, each time with a new value for k. The **Next** statement increases the value of k and causes repeated jumps to the **For** statement until k exceeds its final assigned value of 5. When this happens, control passes to whatever statement follows the **Next** statement.

One of our earlier programs, EXAMPLE2.VBP, has been modified below to use a **For...Next** loop.

```
Private Sub Command1_Click ()      ' Example10

' Declare variables.
Dim intNumber, intCounter As Integer
Dim dblSum, dblAverage As Double
```

```
intNumber = Val(InputBox("How many numbers?"))

    For intCounter = 1 To intNumber
      dblSum = dblSum + Val(InputBox("Enter a number"))
    Next

dblAverage = dblSum / intNumber

Print "You entered " & intNumber & " numbers "
Print "Average is "; Format(dblAverage, "Standard")
Print

End Sub
```

As it stands, the above code will work as long as numerical input is entered from the keyboard. When the program is run, the variable intNumber is assigned a value from an InputBox, which is the total number of entries to be made. A **For...Next** loop is set up which loops the number of times specified in the intNumber variable. Within the loop, each number is read and accumulated into the variable dblSum. Once the loop is completed, variable dblSum holds the summation of all the numbers. The **Print** statements produce the output to the window. Note the **Format** statement which forces the result variable dblAverage to output to 2 decimal places.

## Use of Step

In the last example, as the **Step** modifier was equal to +1 it was omitted. If the step value desired is not equal to +1, the **Step** modifier must be included, as in the next small program.

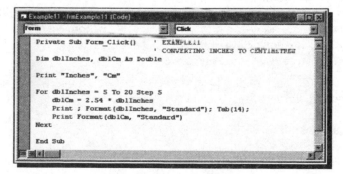

Fig. 6.2 Code for Example11

This will convert 5, 10, 15 and 20 inches into centimetres, in other words, in steps of 5. The output should be as follows:

```
Inches     Cm
  5.00    12.70
 10.00    25.40
 15.00    38.10
 20.00    50.80
```

A negative **Step** modifier is also legal in Visual Basic. For example, the code

```
FOR J = 5 TO 1 STEP -1
    PRINT J
NEXT
```

will print the values 5, 4, 3, 2 and 1.

For positive step values, the loop is executed as long as the control variable is less than or equal to its final value. For negative step values the loop continues as long as the control variable is greater than or equal to its final value.

## Nested For...Next Loops

**For...Next** statements can be nested to allow the programming of loops within loops as shown in the example below:

```
Private Sub Form_DblClick ()    ' EXMPLE12
                                ' Nested FOR-NEXT loops

Dim K, L As Integer

For K = 1 To 9
    For L = K To 9
        Print ; Format(L, "#");
    Next L
    Print
Next K

End Sub
```

When this program is run, two loops are set up as follows:

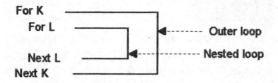

The outer loop is initialised with K=1 and, immediately, the inner, nested loop is executed 9 times. Then the control variable K is incremented by 1, so that now K=2 and the nested loop is executed 8 times. This is repeated until K is equal to 9, when the nested loop is executed only once.

The output of this program is as follows:

```
123456789
23456789
3456789
456789
56789
6789
789
89
9
```

The semicolon after the variable L in the Print statement allows output to be printed close together on the same line. However, each line of print must be terminated with a line feed (that is, it must send the computer display to the next line). This is provided here by the empty Print statement. Without it, all the numbers now appearing on different lines would be printed on the same line.

It is sometimes considered bad programming practice to exit a **For...Next** loop which has not been completed. The results may be unpredictable if you do. However, if such an exit is needed, then make sure you use the **Exit For** command (more about this later).

# The Do Loop

The **Do** loop provides a method of looping through a block of statements and has several variations; it can either check the condition after or before executing the block of statements.

## The Do...Loop Until Configuration

In this configuration the **Do** marks the beginning of the loop, while the **Loop Until** marks the end. Any statements between the **Do** and its corresponding **Loop Until** will be executed repeatedly until the trailer of the **Loop Until** statement is true.

To illustrate using this loop configuration, enter the program below:

```
Private Sub Form_DblClick ()      ' EXAMPLE13

Dim dblValue, dblPercent, dblNum As Double

dblNum = Val(InputBox("Enter number (-1 to END) "))

Do
    dblPercent = Val(InputBox("Enter % "))
    dblValue = dblNum * dblPercent / 100

    Print ; Format(dblPercent, "###.0") & " % of ";
    Print ; Format(dblNum, "#,###.00") & " = ";
    Print ; Format(dblValue, "###.00")
    Print

    dblNum = Val(InputBox("Enter number (-1 to END) "))

Loop Until dblNum < 0

End Sub
```

All statements between the **Do** and **Loop Until** lines are repeated until the trailer of **Until** is true (that is, until you type a negative value in response to the prompt "Enter number..").

Note that

*   In this case, the condition is checked after the statements in the block have been executed at least once. Therefore typing −1 the first time round will not end the program.

*   These programs make use of the 'user defined' formats mentioned in the previous chapter and Appendix C.

## The Do Until...Loop Configuration

In this configuration the loop repeats the block of statements as long as a certain condition is true. For example, the above program can be rewritten as:

```
Private Sub Form_DblClick ()        ' EXAMPLE14

Dim dblValue, dblPercent, dblNum As Double

dblNum = Val(InputBox("Enter number (-1 to END) "))

Do Until dblNum < 0
    dblPercent = Val(InputBox("Enter % "))
    dblValue = dblNum * dblPercent / 100

    Print ; Format(dblPercent, "##0.0") & " % of ";
    Print ; Format(dblNum, "#,##0.00") & " = ";
    Print ; Format(dblValue, "##0.00")
    Print

    dblNum = Val(InputBox("Enter number (-1 to END) "))

Loop

End Sub
```

Here, typing −1 the first time round, ends the program.

## The Do...Loop While Configuration

In this loop configuration, the **While** statement can be used in place of the **Until** statement, provided the relational test has been replaced by its opposite. For example the EXAMPLE13 program will have to be changed to that shown next, to produce the same logical behaviour.

Note that the relational test has been changed from less than zero (<0) to greater or equal to zero (>=0). These and other relational operators will be discussed shortly.

```
Private Sub Form_DblClick ()     ' EXAMPLE15

Dim dblValue, dblPercent, dblNum As Double

dblNum = Val(InputBox("Enter number (-1 to END) "))

Do

    dblPercent = Val(InputBox("Enter % "))
    dblValue = dblNum * dblPercent / 100

    Print ; Format(dblPercent, "##0.0") & " % of ";
    Print ; Format(dblNum, "#,##0.00") & " = ";
    Print ; Format(dblValue, "##0.00")
    Print

    dblNum = Val(InputBox("Enter number (-1 to END) "))

Loop While dblNum >= 0

End Sub
```

## The Do While...Loop Configuration

Similarly, the EXAMPLE14 program will have to be changed to

```
Private Sub Form_DblClick ()     ' EXAMPLE16

Dim dblValue, dblPercent, dblNum As Double

dblNum = Val(InputBox("Enter number (-1 to END) "))

Do While dblNum >= 0
    dblPercent = Val(InputBox("Enter % "))
    dblValue = dblNum * dblPercent / 100

    Print ; Format(dblPercent, "##0.0") & " % of ";
    Print ; Format(dblNum, "#,##0.00") & " = ";
    Print ; Format(dblValue, "##0.00")
    Print

    dblNum = Val(InputBox("Enter number (-1 to END) "))

Loop

End Sub
```

to produce the same logical behaviour as the program from which it was derived.

# The For Each...Next Loop

A **For Each...Next** loop is similar to a **For...Next** loop, but it repeats a group of statements for each element in a collection of objects or in an array, instead of repeating the statements a specified number of times. This is especially helpful if you don't know how many elements are in a collection.

Here is the syntax for the **For Each...Next** loop:

```
For Each element In group
    statements
Next element
```

This statement type is actually a little advanced for our present text. The following example is given on the MSDN Help page, in which a Sub procedure opens a database file Biblio.mdb and adds the name of each table to a list box.

```
Sub ListTableDefs()                    ' EXAMPLE17

    Dim objDb As Database
    Dim MyTableDef As TableDef

    Set objDb = OpenDatabase("c:\vb\biblio.mdb", _
    True, False)

    For Each MyTableDef In objDb.TableDefs()
        List1.AddItem MyTableDef.Name
    Next MyTableDef

End Sub
```

## The Line-Continuation Character

Note the ' _' line-continuation character sequence (a space followed by an underscore), used at the end of the **Set** line in the above code. In the Visual Basic code editor you can break a long statement into multiple lines in the Code window using this line-continuation character.

# The While...Wend Loop

The **While...Wend** loop is another possible configuration, available in enhanced versions of BASIC, so included in Visual Basic for compatibility. It is of the general form:

```
While   <relational test is true>
    { execute this }
    {   block of   }
    { statements   }
Wend
```

This loop configuration produces the same logical behaviour as that of the **Do While...Loop**. In order to illustrate the point, the EXAMPLE16 program is rewritten below with appropriate changes included.

We strongly suggest that you make the suggested changes to these programs and verify for yourself that they work as they should.

```
Private Sub Form_DblClick ()      ' EXAMPLE18

Dim dblValue, dblPercent, dblNum As Double

dblNum = Val(InputBox("Enter number (-1 to END) "))

While dblNum >= 0
    dblPercent = Val(InputBox("Enter % "))
    dblValue = dblNum * dblPercent / 100

    Print ; Format(dblPercent, "##0.0") & " % of ";
    Print ; Format(dblNum, "#,##0.00") & " = ";
    Print ; Format(dblValue, "##0.00")
    Print

    dblNum = Val(InputBox("Enter number (-1 to END) "))

Wend

End Sub
```

# The If Statement

The **IF** statement allows conditional program branching. To illustrate the point, edit the EXAMPLE13 program to:

```
Private Sub Form_DblClick ()      ' EXAMPLE19

Dim dblValue, dblPercent, dblNum As Double

Do
     dblNum = Val(InputBox("Enter number (-1 to END) "))
     If dblNum <0 Then End

     dblPercent = Val(InputBox("Enter % "))
     dblValue = dblNum * dblPercent / 100

     Print ; Format(dblPercent, "##0.0") & " % of ";
     Print ; Format(dblNum, "#,##0.00") & " = ";
     Print ; Format(dblValue, "##0.00")
     Print

     dblNum = Val(InputBox("Enter number (-1 to END) "))

Loop Until dblNum < 0

End Sub
```

When this program is run, you can stop execution by simply entering −1 in response to the "Enter number" prompt. When the **If** statement is encountered, the value of variable dblNum is compared with the constant appearing after the relational operator (<). If the test condition is met, the trailer of the **If** statement is executed (in this case **End**). If, however, the test condition is not met, the next statement after the **If** statement is executed (the dblPercent input statement).

**Note:** The inclusion of the **If...Then** statement in the form adopted above, has made the trailer of the **Loop Until** statement (dblNum < 0) redundant; it merely acts as a device to force looping. In such cases we could use any variable as trailer. We could, for example, use

```
Loop Until False
```

This will cause repeated looping, provided the variable used as trailer is set to zero. If it has any other value, looping will halt.

## Relational Operators within If Statements

The table below shows the relational operators allowed within an **If** statement.

_____**Relational Operators**_____

| Symbol | Example | Meaning |
|--------|---------|---------|
| = | A = B | A equal to B |
| < | A < B | A less than B |
| <= | A <= B | A less than or equal to B |
| > | A > B | A greater than B |
| >= | A >= B | A greater than or equal to B |
| <> | A <> B | A not equal to B |

The power of the **If** statement is increased considerably by the combination of several relational expressions with the logical operators

```
AND   OR   XOR   NOT   EQV   and   IMP
```

We can write the statement

```
If X > 3 And M = 5 Then
```

which states that only if both relational tests are met will the trailer of the **If** statement be executed.

Another example is

```
If X > 3 Or M = 5 Then
```

which states that when either or both relational test(s) are true, then the trailer of the **If** statement will be executed, while the statement

```
If X > 3 Xor M = 5 Then
```

states that when either relational test is true, but not both, then the trailer of the **If** statement will be executed. Finally, the statement

```
If Not (X < 12) Then
```

has the same effect as '**If** X>=12 **Then**' in which the relational test is the negation of that in the above.

# The If...Then...Else Statement

In many cases we have to perform an **IF** statement twice over to detect which of two similar conditions is true. This is illustrated below.

```
Private Sub Form_DblClick ()        ' EXAMPLE20
                                    ' The two IF statements
Dim dblNum As Double

dblNum = Val(InputBox("Enter number between 1 - 99 "))
If dblNum < 10 Then
    Print "One digit number"
End If

If dblNum > 9 Then
    Print "Two digit number"
End If

End Sub
```

A more advanced version of the **If** statement allows both actions to be inserted in its trailer. An example of this is incorporated in the modified program below:

```
Private Sub Form_DblClick ()        ' EXAMPLE21
                        ' IF..THEN..ELSE statements
Dim dblNum As Double

dblNum = Val(InputBox("Enter number between 1 - 99 "))

If dblNum < 10 Then
    Print "One digit number"
Else
    Print "Two digit number"
End If

End Sub
```

Save this program under the filename *EXAMPLE21.VBP* and run it, supplying numbers between 1 and 99. Obviously, if you type in numbers greater than 99 the program will not function correctly in its present form. But assuming that you have obeyed the message and typed, say 50, the second **Print** statement in the trailer of the **If** statement (after the **Else**) will be executed. If the number entered was less than 10, the first **Print** statement after **Then** would be executed. The general structure of this block **If** is:

```
If   <relational test> Then
     { execute this }
     {   block of   }
     {  statements  }
     {   if true    }
Else
     { execute this }
     {   block of   }
     {  statements  }
     {   if false   }
End If
```

Note: In the above structure, no statements can follow the words **Then** and **Else**.

## The ElseIf Statement

If your programming logic requires the use of the block **If** statement to choose amongst several options by, say, using:

```
If   <relational test_1> Then
     { execute this }
     {     block     }
     {    if true    }
Else
     If   <relational test_2> Then
      { execute this }
      {     block     }
      {    if true    }
     Else
      { execute this }
      {     block     }
      {    if false   }
     End If
End If
```

then you can use the **ElseIf** statement to simplify the structure of your program to the following:

```
If   <relational test_1> Then
     { execute this }
     {     block    }
     {    if true   }
     ElseIf   <relational test_2> Then
     { execute this }
     {     block    }
     {    if true   }
     Else
     { execute this }
     {     block    }
     {    if false  }
End If
```

The **ElseIf** statement makes the whole structure much easier
to understand.

## Simple Data Sorting

The program below allows us to enter two numbers, then it tests to find out which is the larger of the two and prints them in descending order. It also illustrates some of the points mentioned in this chapter.

```
Private Sub Form_DblClick ()          ' EXAMPLE22
                                       ' 2 number sort
Dim dblNum1, dblNum2 As Double

Do
    dblNum1 = Val(InputBox("Enter number [-1 to end]"))
    dblNum2 = Val(InputBox("Enter second number"))

    If dblNum1 = -1 Then
       MsgBox "Operation finished"
       End
    ElseIf dblNum1 >= dblNum2 Then
       Print dblNum1, dblNum2
    Else
       Print dblNum2, dblNum1
    End If
Loop Until False

End Sub
```

The program can be stopped by entering –1 for dblNum1. Otherwise, dblNum1 is compared with dblNum2 and the appropriate Print statement is executed.

The sorting problem becomes more complicated, however, if instead of two numbers we introduce a third one. For two number sorting we had two possible Print statements (the number of possible permutations being 1*2=2. For three number sorting however, the total number of Print statements becomes six (the total possible permutations being equal to 1*2*3=6. With numbers A, B and C, the combinations are (A,B,C), (A,C,B), (C,A,B), (C,B,A), (B,C,A) and (B,A,C). Thus, if we were to pursue the suggested logic in dealing with the problem it would result in a very inefficient program.

Here is a way in which, with only two **If** statements and one **Print** statement, the same solution to the three-number sorting problem can be achieved. It uses a different logic and it is explained here with the help of three imaginary playing cards, shown in Fig. 6.3 below.

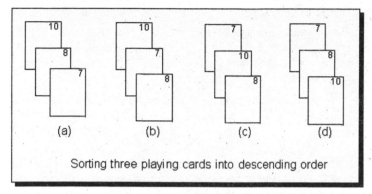

Sorting three playing cards into descending order

Fig. 6.3 Sorting Three Cards

Assume that you are holding these cards in your hand and you wish to arrange them in descending order. Look at the front two (a) and arrange them so that the highest value appears in front. Now look at the back two (b) and arrange them so that the highest of these two is now in front. Obviously, if the highest card had been at the back, in the first instance, it would by now have moved to the middle position, as shown in (c), so a repeat of the whole procedure is necessary to ensure that the highest card is at the front (d).

The program below achieves this.

```
Private Sub Form_DblClick ()        ' EXAMPLE23
                        ' 3 number descending sort
Dim A, B, C, dblTemp As Double

A = Val(InputBox("Enter first number"))
B = Val(InputBox("Enter second number"))
C = Val(InputBox("Enter third number"))
```

```
Do While A < B Or B < C
    If A < B Then
        dblTemp = A
        A = B
        B = dblTemp
    End If
    If B < C Then
        dblTemp = B
        B = C
        C = dblTemp
    End If
Loop
Print A, B, C

End Sub
```

The following actions are indicated: If the value in A is less than that in B, exchange them so that the value of A is now stored in B and the value of B is now stored in A.

Note, however, that were we to put the value of B into A, we should lose the number stored in A (by overwriting). We therefore transfer the contents of A to the temporary variable dblTemp, then transfer the contents of B to A and finally transfer the contents of dblTemp to B.

The second rotation, necessary when B is less than C, is achieved in a similar manner. The whole process is repeated (with the help of the **Do While...Loop** statement), for as long as both A is less than B, or B is less than C. Type this program into the computer under the filename EXAMPLE23.VBP.

# The Select Case Statement

This is a statement which allows program action to be made dependent on the value of a variable, or an expression. It is Visual Basic's aid to writing readable programs and provides an efficient alternative to multiple **If** statements. The general form of the statement is written as follows:

```
Select Case Expression
   Case A
     { execute these }
     {  statement(s) }
   Case B To D
     { execute these }
     {  statement(s) }
   Case E,X
     { execute these }
     {  statement(s) }
   Case Else
     { execute these }
     {  statement(s) }
End Select
```

where Expression can evaluate to either a number or a string.
A particular **Case** statement within the block (for example,
CASE A), will be executed only if Expression evaluates to a
constant or a string represented by A.

The following examples will help to illustrate using the **Select
Case** structure. The first and simpler one, looks for input in the
form of a number representing the day of the week (Monday 1,
Tuesday 2, etc.). It then evaluates this intDayNum variable
(which is the Expression in the general format) to a constant,
as follows:

```
Private Sub Form_DblClick ()      ' EXAMPLE24

Dim intDayNum As Integer

intDayNum = Val(InputBox("Enter day number (1-7) "))

Select Case intDayNum
    Case 1 To 5
        Print "Working day"
    Case 6, 7
        Print "Weekend"
    Case Else
        Print "Not a day"
End Select

End Sub
```

The second example (based on one in the Help system), is a bit more complicated. You should make sure you understand how it works, as several keyboard entry error trapping methods are also introduced.

```
Sub Form_Click ()           ' EXAMPLE25

Dim Msg, UserInput          ' Declare variables

Msg = "Enter a letter, or a number between 0 and 9."

UserInput = InputBox(Msg)   ' Get user input

If Not IsNumeric(UserInput) Then   ' Check input type
    If Len(UserInput) <> 0 Then
        Select Case Asc(UserInput)  ' If a letter
        Case 65 To 90    ' Must be uppercase.
            Msg = "You entered the uppercase letter '"
            Msg = Msg & Chr(Asc(UserInput)) & "'."

        Case 97 To 122   ' Must be lowercase.
            Msg = "You entered the lower-case letter '"
            Msg = Msg & Chr(Asc(UserInput)) & "'."

        Case Else    ' Must be something else.
            Msg = "Not a letter or number."
        End Select
    End If
Else
        Select Case CDbl(UserInput) ' If a number.
        Case 1, 3, 5, 7, 9  ' It's odd.
            Msg = UserInput & " is an odd number."
        Case 0, 2, 4, 6, 8  ' It's even.
            Msg = UserInput & " is an even number."
        Case Else    ' Out of range.
            Msg = "You entered a number outside "
            Msg = Msg & "the requested range."
        End Select
End If

    MsgBox Msg   ' Display message
End Sub
```

In the first **If** statement, the expression **Not IsNumeric** only accepts letters as input, not numbers. If the input is a number, control passes to the **Else** statement.

In line 7, **Asc** returns a numeric value that is the ANSI code for the letter entered (see table in next chapter). The **Case** statements then act depending on these numeric codes. The first one accepts uppercase letters (which have ANSI codes in the range 65 to 90). The second one accepts lowercase letters (which have ANSI codes in the range 97 to 122).

In line 10, the part of the expression **Chr(Asc...** changes the ANSI code back to the original character, so that it can be displayed in a message box.

The function **CDbl** in the second **Select Case** expression, explicitly converts the data type to Double precision. The following two **Case** statements select between odd and even numbers. Anything that reaches the final **Case Else** statement is neither a letter, or a number between 1 and 9, so is flagged as such.

# Data Type Conversion

The **CDbl** function in the last example explicitly converted an expression from one data type to another. Visual Basic has 7 such functions to enable conversion to all the types of data. The syntax is

```
CType(expression)
```

Where *CType* is one of the functions from the list below and expression can be any valid string, or numeric expression.

| Function | Converts to: |
| --- | --- |
| CVar | Variant |
| CCur | Currency |
| CDbl | Double |
| CInt | Integer |
| CLng | Long |
| CSng | Single |
| CStr | String |

You can use these data type conversion functions to ensure that the result of a calculation is expressed as a particular data type rather than the normal data type of the result.

# Exiting Block Structures

If, for any reason, you require to exit a loop, a function or a procedure prematurely (for example when a data search for a match is successful), then use one of the following:

```
Exit Do
Exit For
Exit Function
Exit Sub
```

the first two being used to exit loops, and the last two to exit functions and procedures.

# 7

# Strings and Arrays

## String Variables

In Visual Basic, string variables can be distinguished from numeric variables by including the $ tag after their name, or more usually, by declaring them as such in a Dimension statement, such as:

```
Dim strA As String
```

By default, a string variable has a flexible length. It gets longer, or shorter, as you assign different data to it. To fix its length you can add the required size to the statement:

```
Dim strA As String * 25
```

In this case strA will always be allocated 25 characters of storage space. If it does not need this length it will be 'padded' with trailing spaces. If the data it holds is longer than 25 characters it will be truncated (and some will be lost).

If a variable is not declared in a program it takes the default **Variant** type, which is a special data type that can contain numeric, string, date, or currency data.

## ANSI Character Codes

Visual Basic assigns a numeric code to each character on the keyboard, according to the ANSI (American National Standards Institute) code, as shown in the tables overleaf. Thus, each letter of the alphabet is assigned a numeric value. The first 128 characters (0 - 127) are common with the ASCII set used in most DOS applications.

## Table 1 of ANSI Conversion Codes

| | | | | | | | |
|---|---|---|---|---|---|---|---|
| 0 | • | 32 | [space] | 64 | @ | 96 | ` |
| 1 | • | 33 | ! | 65 | A | 97 | a |
| 2 | • | 34 | " | 66 | B | 98 | b |
| 3 | • | 35 | # | 67 | C | 99 | c |
| 4 | • | 36 | $ | 68 | D | 100 | d |
| 5 | • | 37 | % | 69 | E | 101 | e |
| 6 | • | 38 | & | 70 | F | 102 | f |
| 7 | • | 39 | ' | 71 | G | 103 | g |
| 8 | * * | 40 | ( | 72 | H | 104 | h |
| 9 | * * | 41 | ) | 73 | I | 105 | i |
| 10 | * * | 42 | * | 74 | J | 106 | j |
| 11 | • | 43 | + | 75 | K | 107 | k |
| 12 | • | 44 | , | 76 | L | 108 | l |
| 13 | * * | 45 | - | 77 | M | 109 | m |
| 14 | • | 46 | . | 78 | N | 110 | n |
| 15 | • | 47 | / | 79 | O | 111 | o |
| 16 | • | 48 | 0 | 80 | P | 112 | p |
| 17 | • | 49 | 1 | 81 | Q | 113 | q |
| 18 | • | 50 | 2 | 82 | R | 114 | r |
| 19 | • | 51 | 3 | 83 | S | 115 | s |
| 20 | • | 52 | 4 | 84 | T | 116 | t |
| 21 | • | 53 | 5 | 85 | U | 117 | u |
| 22 | • | 54 | 6 | 86 | V | 118 | v |
| 23 | • | 55 | 7 | 87 | W | 119 | w |
| 24 | • | 56 | 8 | 88 | X | 120 | x |
| 25 | • | 57 | 9 | 89 | Y | 121 | y |
| 26 | • | 58 | : | 90 | Z | 122 | z |
| 27 | • | 59 | ; | 91 | [ | 123 | { |
| 28 | • | 60 | < | 92 | \ | 124 | | |
| 29 | • | 61 | = | 93 | ] | 125 | } |
| 30 | • | 62 | > | 94 | ^ | 126 | ~ |
| 31 | • | 63 | ? | 95 | _ | 127 | • |

•     Characters not supported by Microsoft Windows.

* *    Values 8, 9, 10, and 13, above, convert to backspace, tab, linefeed, and carriage return respectively and can be used in programs to create these actions.

_____**Table 2 of ANSI Conversion Codes**_____

| 128 | • | 160 | [space] | 192 | À | 224 | à |
|-----|---|-----|---------|-----|---|-----|---|
| 129 | • | 161 | ¡ | 193 | Á | 225 | á |
| 130 | • | 162 | ¢ | 194 | Â | 226 | â |
| 131 | • | 163 | £ | 195 | Ã | 227 | ã |
| 132 | • | 164 | ¤ | 196 | Ä | 228 | ä |
| 133 | • | 165 | ¥ | 197 | Å | 229 | å |
| 134 | • | 166 | ¦ | 198 | Æ | 230 | æ |
| 135 | • | 167 | § | 199 | Ç | 231 | ç |
| 136 | • | 168 | ¨ | 200 | È | 232 | è |
| 137 | • | 169 | © | 201 | É | 233 | é |
| 138 | • | 170 | ª | 202 | Ê | 234 | ê |
| 139 | • | 171 | « | 203 | Ë | 235 | ë |
| 140 | • | 172 | ¬ | 204 | Ì | 236 | ì |
| 141 | • | 173 | - | 205 | Í | 237 | í |
| 142 | • | 174 | ® | 206 | Î | 238 | î |
| 143 | • | 175 | ‾ | 207 | Ï | 239 | ï |
| 144 | • | 176 | ° | 208 | Ð | 240 | ð |
| 145 | • | 177 | ± | 209 | Ñ | 241 | ñ |
| 146 | • | 178 | ² | 210 | Ò | 242 | ò |
| 147 | • | 179 | ³ | 211 | Ó | 243 | ó |
| 148 | • | 180 | ´ | 212 | Ô | 244 | ô |
| 149 | • | 181 | µ | 213 | Õ | 245 | õ |
| 150 | • | 182 | ¶ | 214 | Ö | 246 | ö |
| 151 | • | 183 | · | 215 | × | 247 | ÷ |
| 152 | • | 184 | ¸ | 216 | Ø | 248 | ø |
| 153 | • | 185 | ¹ | 217 | Ù | 249 | ù |
| 154 | • | 186 | º | 218 | Ú | 250 | ú |
| 155 | • | 187 | » | 219 | Û | 251 | û |
| 156 | • | 188 | ¼ | 220 | Ü | 252 | ü |
| 157 | • | 189 | ½ | 221 | Ý | 253 | ý |
| 158 | • | 190 | ¾ | 222 | Þ | 254 | þ |
| 159 | • | 191 | ¿ | 223 | ß | 255 | ÿ |

**Note:** The codes within the range 128 to 255 above contain a series of special characters that are not on the standard keyboard. These include international and accented letters, fractions and currency symbols.

As with numbers, strings can be assigned to variables in several ways. For example, the code below assigns a string to the variable named strA and then prints strA to the current window.

```
strA = "ABC123"
Print strA
```

When the code is run, Visual Basic outputs

```
ABC123
```

By default, when strings appear in an **If** statement, they are compared character by character from left to right on the basis of the ANSI values until a difference is found. For example, if a character in a position in StrA has a higher ANSI code than the character in the same position in StrB, then StrA is greater than StrB. If all the characters in the same positions are identical but one string has more characters than the other, the longer string is the greater of the two. Thus, strings of letters can be placed easily in alphabetical order and sorted lists of names, etc., are possible.

In Visual Basic, however, the Option Compare statement effects the evaluation of string comparisons.

## Option Compare (Binary | Text)

This statement controls the way string comparisons are performed. When the *Binary* option is specified comparisons are performed in the default manner as described above. The *Text* option causes the comparisons to be case insensitive, and no distinction is made between upper and lower case letters during comparisons (in other words, "A" = "a").

The **Option Compare** statement must appear before any procedures in a code module and will only effect the comparisons in the module in which it appears. If no Option Compare statement is present in a module, the default comparison option of *Binary* is used.

## StrComp(*strA, strB*[, *compare*])

This function compares *strA* with *strB*, using the comparison mode specified in (*compare*) and returns an integer value. If *compare* is not provided, the current **Option Compare** mode is used. This function allows you to override the current Option Compare mode for an individual string comparison.

# String Functions

In the statements given so far, the string variables have been considered in their entirety. We shall now introduce some functions which give access to any character within a given string and hence allow manipulation of that string.

## Left and Left$ Functions

These both return a number of characters from the left of a string argument. The function is used as follows:

```
Left[$](StrA, n)
```

and will return the leftmost n characters of StrA. When used without the $ suffix, **Left** returns a Variant; whereas **Left$** returns a String. In most cases you are probably better off adding the $ and declaring all your string variables as such.

## Right and Right$ Functions

These work in exactly the same way as the **Left[$]** functions, but they return the rightmost characters of the specified string.

## Mid and Mid$ Functions

In the same way, these return a Variant or String from part of a source string, as follows:

```
Mid[$](StrA, Start[, Length])
```

Where Start and Length are numbers. In this case the string with Length number of characters and beginning at position Start of StrA will be returned.

If Length is omitted, the **Mid[$]** function returns all the characters from the start position to the end of the string.

## Other String Functions

There are a few more functions that help with string manipulation, many of which will be demonstrated in later examples.

The **Len**(StrA) function is used to find the number of characters in StringA.

The **InStr**([Start,] StrA, StrB) function returns the location of StrB in StrA, optionally beginning the search Start characters into the string. If Start is omitted the search will begin at the first character. This function is very useful for locating spaces between words in a string.

**Space$**(Num) will create a string with Num spaces in it, and **String$**(Num, "X") will create a string consisting of Num characters of type X. If a number is used for X the ANSI code character will be used. The first is useful, with no number to place spaces between words being built in a string expression, the second for building lines with graphic type characters.

**Ucase$**(StrA) and **Lcase$**(StrA) convert all the characters in StrA to upper, or lower, case respectively. An example of their use is to convert keyboard entry characters before testing for the entry. Otherwise you would have to test for both upper and lower case letters.

The best way to understand these functions is by entering and playing with an example; so build the Form shown in Fig. 7.1.

This small program doesn't really serve any great purpose. It expects you to enter your first and last names into the top text box **separated by a space**. Clicking the **Go** button then places the two parts of the name into their respective text boxes. The **Clear** button resets the boxes and **Quit** exits the program.

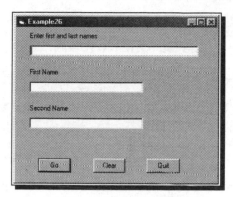

Fig. 7.1 Example26 Form in Run Mode

The form has 3 Text boxes, with a Label placed above each, and 3 Command buttons, as shown. You may have to go back to the earlier chapters if you need help setting these up. Set the following object Properties as shown below, but leave the others with the default settings.

| Object | Property | Setting |
|---|---|---|
| Command1 | Caption | Go |
| | Default* | True |
| | Name | CmdGo |
| Command2 | Caption | Clear |
| | Name | CmdClear |
| Command3 | Caption | Quit |
| | Cancel* | True |
| | Name | CmdQuit |
| Label1 | Caption | Enter first and last names |
| Label2 | Caption | First Name |
| Label3 | Caption | Last Name |
| Text1 | TabIndex | 0 |
| | Text | Cleared |
| Text2 | Text | Cleared |
| Text3 | Text | Cleared |

* See end of example for more explanation.

When you have finished the above Property changes, double click the background of the form and enter the declaration statement below into the **(General) (Declarations)** section.

Fig. 7.2 The General Declarations for Example26

The **Option Explicit** statement should be placed there automatically, as long as you have followed our recommendations on page 26. If not, why not go back and do it now. The **Dim** statement allows the variable strInput to be used from any of the form's commands.

Then double-click the Text1 box on the form and enter the following code, making sure it is entered into the Change procedure code window. This will then be actioned whenever the text entered into the box is changed at run time.

```
Private Sub Text1_Change ()
    strInput = Text1.Text
End Sub
```

The main code to work the program is next entered in the code window of the Go Command button.

```
Private Sub CmdGo_Click ()

Dim LWord, Msg, Rword, SpacePos   ' Declare variables.

 SpacePos = InStr(1, strInput, " ")   ' Find the space.
 If SpacePos Then
    LWord = Left(strInput, SpacePos - 1)
    Rword = Right(strInput, Len(strInput) - SpacePos)
    Text2.Text = UCase$(LWord) ' First name
    Text3.Text = UCase$(Rword) ' Last name
 Else
    Msg = "You didn't enter two words."
    MsgBox Msg   ' Display error message.
    Text1.Text = ""   ' Clear text box
```

```
      Text1.SetFocus   ' Place insertion point in box
   End If

End Sub
```

In the Click procedure code window of the Clear Command button, enter the following code which clears the text boxes and places the insertion point in the first, ready for input.

```
Private Sub CmdClear_Click ()

Text1.Text = ""
Text1.SetFocus
Text2.Text = ""
Text3.Text = ""

End Sub
```

Last of all, place the one word of code in the Quit Command button code window as follows:

```
Private Sub CmdQuit_Click ()
    End 'Close program
End Sub
```

The logic of the code 'behind' the Go button should be fairly easy to follow. Four local variables are first declared, which are only used in this subroutine. The **Instr** function then looks for a space (" ") in the entered text held in the variable strInput (short for User Input string).

If a space is found, the lines under the **If** statement are actioned. The first and last names are cut out of the strInput string and then converted to upper case.

If no space character is found, the **Else** statements are actioned. An error message is placed on the screen, the input text box is cleared and the focus is placed back into it to receive correct input.

Two of the Properties set in this example need more comment. The Quit Command button property *Cancel* was set to True. This controls the action of the <Esc> key in the program. With this setting, pressing the <Esc> key is the same as clicking this button. The Go Command button property *Default* was also set to True. This controls the action of the <Enter> key. Pressing this key then has the same effect as clicking the Go button.

# String Conversion Functions

There are four additional string functions in Visual Basic:

```
ASC( ), CHR$( ), STR$( ) and VAL( )
```

Examples of these functions are given next.

## ANSI Conversion

Using the **ASC** function in the statement

```
N = ASC("ABCD")
```

will return the ANSI code for the first character of the string enclosed in the brackets of the function. In this case, 65 will be returned (see Table on ANSI Conversion Codes). The function name ASC actually refers to ASCII code conversion as used in previous DOS versions of Basic. But all the usual keyboard codes are the same in both codes, so the name has been kept in Visual Basic to maintain compatibility with code written for earlier versions.

## Character Conversion

Using the **CHR$** function in the statement

```
C$ = CHR$(66)
```

will return the ANSI character that corresponds to the value of the argument, in this case the letter B. The value of the argument must lie between 0 and 255.

## String Conversion

Using the **STR$** function in the statement

```
S$ = STR$(X)
```

will convert the value of the argument into a string. X is a numeric variable which might be the result of a calculation. In this case, if X had the numerical value of 98.56, say, then S$ would be converted to the string "98.56".

## Value of String

If R$ represents a string given by

```
R$ = "3.123E12 metres"
```

then the statement

```
X = VAL(R$)
```

will return the value of the string up to the first non-numeric character, in this case 3.123E+12. If the string begins with a non-numeric character then the value 0 is returned.

## String Concatenation

Visual Basic allows the concatenation, or joining together, of strings. We shall illustrate this facility by considering the following program in which the computer asks you to enter your surname first, followed by your first name. It then concatenates the two (first name first followed by surname with a space in between) and prints the result which is held in string variable strOutput.

```
Private Sub Form_Click ()   ' EXAMPLE27

Dim strSName, strFName, strName, strOutput As String

strSName = InputBox$("Enter SURNAME please")
strFName = InputBox$("Enter FIRST NAME please")
strName = UCase$(strFName) + Space$(1) + UCase$(strSName)

strOutput = "HELLO " & strName
Print strOutput

End Sub
```

As it stands, the program is rather trivial. However, using concatenation together with some of the string functions mentioned earlier, can result in a somewhat more spectacular result.

To illustrate this, delete the Print statement of the above program and replace it with the following lines to the program:

```
FontName = "Courier New"    ' EXAMPLE28
FontSize = 10

Intlength = Len(strName)
If Intlength > 22 Then
 strName = UCase$(Left$(strFName, 1) + ". " + strSName)
 Intlength = Len(strName)
End If
For I = 1 To Intlength
 Print Mid$(strName, I, 1);
 If I = 1 Then Print " "; strName;
    If I = Intlength Then Print " "; strName;
 Print Tab(Intlength + 4); Mid$(strName, I, 1)
Next I
```

Also add the following statement with the other declarations.

```
Dim intLength, I As Integer
```

Run the program and supply it with your full name (surname first). What you would see in the form window, if your name was JOHN BROWN, is shown below. This would not work properly without the line of code setting the printing font to Courier New which is not proportional.

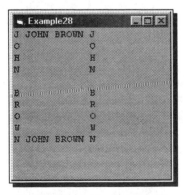

Fig. 7.3 Printout for Example28

Note that the program has worked out the length of your full name and allowed enough space between the two vertical columns to write it horizontally on the first and last rows.

Now Run the program again, but this time type in a really long name, say CHRISTOPHER VERYLONGFELLOW. Can you work out from the program lines and the output on your screen what has happened? Try it.

# Arrays

Some people find difficulty understanding the concept of arrays in programming. An array is a set of sequentially indexed elements of the same type and name, with each element having a unique index number to identify it. Changes made to one element of an array do not affect the other elements.

An array can only store data of the same type. Of course, if the array data type is Variant, then numerical, string and date/time data can all be stored in the same array.

## String Arrays

A number of strings can be stored under a common name in a string array. Let us assume that we have four names, e.g., SMITH, JONES, BROWN and WILSON that we want to store in a string array. In Visual Basic, whenever an array is to be used in a program, you must declare your intention to do so. There are several ways of doing this. One is to place a **Dim** statement, like the one on the next page, into the **(General) (Declarations)** section of a form. This dimensions the array Names() with the elements 1 to 4, and allows the array to be used from any of the form's commands.

```
Dim Names(1 To 4) As String
```

Enter this line into the declarations section of a new project form and then type the following code into the Click procedure:

```
Private Sub Form_Click ()    ' EXAMPLE29
                                   ' Use of a string array

Dim I As Integer
Names(1) = "SMITH"           ' Load array
Names(2) = "JONES"
Names(3) = "BROWN"
Names(4) = "WILSON"

For I = 1 To 4
    Print "Names ("; I; ")",
Next I
Print
For I = 1 To 4
    Print Names(I),
Next I
Print
End Sub
```

When run, this program demonstrates how the 4 elements of the array Names() can be manipulated by using the index number of each element in your code. Any reference to an array name within a program must be of the form

```
Names(I)
```

Another way of dimensioning this array with 4 elements is:

```
Dim Names(4) As String
```

However, the element numbers in this case would be 0 to 3, as unless the range is implicitly declared it starts, by default, from 0. You can, if you want, force the lower 'bound' to 1 by placing the line

```
Option Base 1
```

in the declarations section of your form.


A simple way to visualise a string array is as follows:

| SMITH | JONES | BROWN | WILSON |

The four names are stored in a common box which has four compartments (or elements), each compartment containing one name. Thus, Names(2) refers to the 2nd element of string array Names(), and Names(4) to the 4th element.

# Subscripted Numeric Variables

Array variables are often called subscripted variables and they permit the representation of many quantities with one variable name. A particular quantity is indicated, as we saw above, by writing a subscript in parentheses after the variable name. So an array allows you to use a single variable name for a complete list of related data. Items from the list are located by their index (or subscript) number, which can be referred to as a number, or an expression that results in a number. In Visual Basic an array may have up to 60 dimensions, each one represented by a different subscript.

The elements of a one-dimensional array can be represented as follows:

```
A(0)      A(1)      A(2)      A(3)      A(4)
```

while those of a two-dimensional array as:

```
A(0,0)    A(0,1)    A(0,2)    A(0,3)
A(1,0)    A(1,1)    A(1,2)    A(1,3)
A(2,0)    A(2,1)    A(2,2)    A(2,3)
```

The first of the two subscripts refers to the row number, running from 0 to the maximum number of declared rows, and the second subscript to the column number, running from 0 to the maximum number of declared columns.

A three-dimensional array can be thought of as stacked two-dimensional arrays with the third subscript, running from 0 to the maximum height of the stack. More complex structures follow the same procedures.

As with string arrays, numerical arrays must be declared prior to their use, either with a **Dim** statement placed in the declarations section of a form or module, with a **Global** statement placed in the declarations section of a module, or with a **Static** statement placed in the procedure.

When declared with:

**Global**    an array is available to any form or module contained in a project.

**Dim**    an array is available to any procedure on the form or module on which it is placed.

**Static**    an array is available only within the procedure in which it is declared.

The form of the statement is shown below:

```
Dim X(15), Y(3,5), Z(3,5,4)
Global X(15), Y(3,5), Z(3,5,4)
Static X(15), Y(3,5), Z(3,5,4)
```

where array X() has been declared to be a one-dimensional array with a maximum of 16 elements (don't forget the zero'th element), array Y(,) has been declared as a two-dimensional array of 4 rows and 6 columns, and array Z(,,) as a three-dimensional array of 4 rows and 6 columns stacked 5 deep. The number of arrays that can be declared simultaneously is dependent only on the available memory in your computer. Don't forget that multi-dimensional arrays can very quickly eat into your available memory.

# Static and Dynamic Arrays

Visual Basic allows you to assign a portion of memory for array use in two different ways. These are:

**Static arrays**    When the declaration is made with subscripted variables, for example DIM Year(1980 TO 2000) or DIM Aname(15)

**Dynamic arrays**    When the declaration is made with empty subscript brackets, for example **Dim** Year() or **Dim** Aname()

Static array memory is always the same size for each run of the program and cannot be used for any other purpose.

Dynamic memory is allocated during run time and the space may vary for each run of the program. Dynamic memory can be freed up at any time for other use, with the statement

```
Erase Array_name
```

This command also reinitialises the elements of fixed arrays as well as freeing dynamic array storage space.

Before your program can refer to the dynamic array again, it must re-declare the array variable's dimensions using a **ReDim** statement. However, although dynamic arrays are memory efficient, accessing values held in them may be slightly slower that accessing values held in static arrays.

There are two main error messages which relate to the use of arrays. These are:

```
Subscript out of range
Overflow
```

The first error occurs if an attempt is made to use an array element that is outside the declared dimension, or if an attempt has been made to dimension the array with a negative number of elements. The second error occurs if an attempt is made to use an array for which there is no room in the computer's memory.

As an example of array usage we will build a small stocktaking program. After you have studied it, enter the code as EXMPLE30.VBP.

First declare two arrays in the declarations section of a new project form as follows:

```
Dim Item(4) As String
Dim Stock(4, 2) As Double
```

Then enter the following code into the Click procedure of the form. Note the use of the colon (:) to separate multiple statements on a line. You could enter all the Print statements together on one line if you prefer.

```
Private Sub Form_click ()         ' EXAMPLE30 - Stocktaking

Dim I As Integer, Xname As String
Item(1) = "INK ERASER"              'Load data into arrays
Stock(1, 1) = 200: Stock(1, 2) = .1
Item(2) = "PENCIL ERASER"
Stock(2, 1) = 320: Stock(2, 2) = .15
Item(3) = "TYPING ERASER"
Stock(3, 1) = 25: Stock(3, 2) = .25
Item(4) = "CORRECTION FLUID"
Stock(4, 1) = 150: Stock(4, 2) = .5

Do
 Xname = InputBox$("Which item? 'END' to finish")
 If UCase$(Xname) = "END" Then End
 For I = 1 To 4
    If UCase$(Xname) = Left$(Item(I), 3) Then
       Print Item(I); "  ";
       Print  Stock(I, 1) & " in stock @ ";
              Print Format(Stock(I, 2), "Currency");
       Print " each."
    End If
 Next I
Loop Until False

End Sub
```

When run, the Input Box will only accept an entry whose first three letters are the same as one of the items entered into the Item() array.

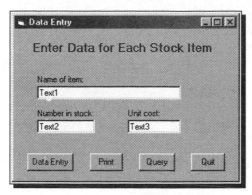

Fig. 7.4 Entry Form for Example31 with Text Boxes Named

The last example included all the data for the arrays in the code. This is not always convenient, so the next one has a front-end data entry form and the user can enter any suitable data at run time.

Form1, shown here in Fig. 7.4, has been given the *Caption* property 'Data Entry'. It has 3 Text Boxes, 4 Command Buttons and several Labels. Open a new project (EXAMPLE31.VBP)

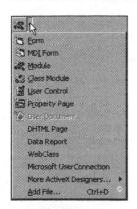

with 2 forms and a Code Module. This is the first time we have used more than one form. Don't panic, simply click the Add Form icon on the Toolbar, shown open in Fig. 7.5, and select **Form** and **Module**. The second form will be used purely as a window to hold our print output, and the module will be used for global declarations of our arrays.

We will leave it to you to build the Form1 entry form on your own. The code for the various objects is shown below.

Fig. 7.5 Add Options

The declarations placed in the new code module are:

```
Option Base 1
Global Item(10) As String
Global Stock(10, 2) As Double
```

Set the TabIndex properties to 0, 1 and 2 for the text boxes Text1, Text2 and Text3 respectively. Then add the code for the 4 command buttons, which have been renamed, as shown below, to cmdEnter, cmdPrint, cmdQuery and cmdQuit.

```
Private Sub cmdEnter_Click()        ' EXAMPLE31
                              ' Improved stocktaking program
Static Counter  As Integer
   If Counter < 1 Then Counter = 1
   Item(Counter) = Text1.Text
   Stock(Counter, 1) = Val(Text2.Text)
   Stock(Counter, 2) = Val(Text3.Text)
   Counter = Counter + 1
   Text1.Text = ""
   Text2.Text = ""
   Text3.Text = ""
   Text1.SetFocus
End Sub
---------------------------
Private Sub cmdPrint_Click()
Dim I As Integer
Form2.Show
For I = 1 To 10
   If Item(I) <> "" Then
        Form2.Print Item(I), Stock(I, 1),
        Form2.Print Format(Stock(I, 2), "Currency")
   End If
Next I
End Sub
---------------------------
Private Sub cmdQuery_Click()
Dim I As Integer, Xname, Msg As String
Do
   Form2.Show
   Msg = "Which item? 'END' to finish"
   Xname = InputBox$(Msg, "Data Query", , 7000, 5000)
   Xname = Left$(Xname, 3)

   For I = 1 To 10
   If UCase$(Xname) = "END" Then Exit Do
   If UCase$(Xname) = UCase$(Left$(Item(I), 3)) Then
```

```
            Form2.Print Item(I); "   ";
            Form2.Print Stock(I, 1) & " in stock @ ";
            Form2.Print Format(Stock(I, 2), "Currency");
            Form2.Print " each."
        End If
        Next I
    Loop Until False
    Form2.Hide
    Form1.Show
    Text1.SetFocus
    End Sub
    ---------------------------
    Private Sub cmdQuit_Click()
    End
    End Sub
```

You should, by now, be able to follow this code quite easily. Remember that if you forget the correct syntax for a command, simply select it in the editing window and press **F1**. As it stands the program will accept 10 sets of data, but would be easy to modify.

The **Static** declaration allows the variable 'Counter' to maintain its value; without this it would be re-set each time the Sub was run.

The statement Form2.Show opens the window Form2 and Form2Hide makes it invisible to the user. The Print statements have to be prefixed with 'Form2.' to force printing onto this window (otherwise it will run behind the features on Form1.

The **InputBox$()** statement has a title as well as X and Y co-ordinates to force the box to the lower right portion of the screen. Otherwise it opens over the Form2 printing window. You must use all the positioning commas, as shown, to get these to work. Good luck!

## Control Arrays

An array can be very useful in Visual Basic with controls. If, for example, you need four command buttons which are related and must be the same size, such as the buttons on a toolbar.

You can create one button then copy it and paste it onto a frame. A message box will inform you that you already have such a control and asks if you would you like to make an array.

If you click the **Yes** button, you can then paste as many buttons as you like, and each will be designated by the name of the first button followed by an index number in brackets, such as cmdToolbar(1), cmdToolbar(2), etc. All arrays start at zero so your original button will now be cmdToolbar(0). This method uses less memory and keeps groups of controls (with a related purpose) into one area.

As an array of command buttons will also have a common click, or mouse move event, you must be careful how you write the code behind them. The most common method is to use a Select Case statement (see page 102). The following is an example of data control related command buttons in an array named cmdData(Index), where Index is the number designating which button we are addressing (beginning with zero for the first button in the array).

```
cmdData_ click()
Select Case Index
    Case 0        'first button in the array
    Data1.recordset.addnew
    Case 1        'second button in the array
    Data1.recordset.delete
    Data1.recordset.movenext
    Case 2
    Data1.recordset.update
End Select
```

The actual commands are not important here, but note how all the database code can now be found in one place. You could also have one error handler for all of the database related buttons.

# 8

# More on Controls

In Chapters 2 and 3, we briefly described the main controls available in Visual Basic, but so far we have not actually used some of them. We have concentrated more on the fundamentals of the programming language behind the controls themselves. Perhaps the easiest way to come to terms with the other controls is to study how the sample program CONTROLS.VBP works. This should have been installed with Visual Basic.

It was located in our set-up in the folder "C:\Program Files\Microsoft Visual Studio\MSDN98\98VSa\1033\SAMPLES\ VB98\Controls" With your version the path may not be the same, but by now you should be able to find it OK. You might also want to look at an overview of the sample program in MSDN Help, as shown in Fig. 8.1 below.

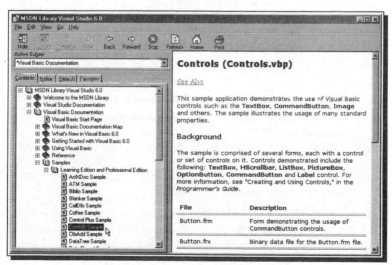

Fig. 8.1 MSDN Help on Visual Basic's Examples

# The CONTROLS.VBP Sample

Load this project and set up your screen as shown in Fig. 8.2. Here, we have opened the frmMain by selecting it in the Project Explorer window and then clicking the **View Object** button.

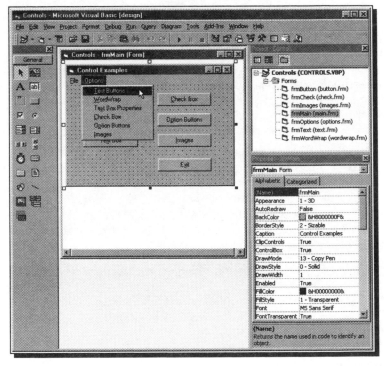

Fig. 8.2 Visual Basic's Controls Example Program

This form has six command buttons and an **Exit** button, which you should be very familiar with; and a menu, shown opened above. The six buttons and the menu give access to the other six forms which make up this project.

If you double-click the frmMain window in design mode and open the **Object** drop-down list you will see reference to all the button and menu code procedures. The screen dump of Fig. 8.3, on the next page, shows this list and a typical Procedure code.

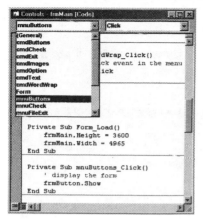

Fig. 8.3 Object Drop Down List

In fact for each menu item, the code simply opens the relevant form window using the **Show** statement.

If you look at the code behind the six command buttons, you will see just one line in each, such as:

```
mnuButtons_Click
```

This is the code in the cmdButtons_Click procedure, which simply activates the relevant menu option.

This is a very easy way to transfer control around the program, and we will look at how to set up menus a little later on. In the meantime, run the program and move between the various options. You will be amazed at what can be produced in Visual Basic with very little in the way of code.

## The Example Files

This **Controls** example program has been included, in one form or another, with all the versions of Visual Basic we have used. By looking at the coding behind the sections of this program, you can learn an awful lot. We strongly recommend you spend several hours doing this.

Hopefully it will be provided with future versions of Visual Basic as well. Just to be on the safe side, though, we have included the source files on the Companion Disc to this book (see inside back cover) and on one of our Web sites. To download the latter, enter the following URL address into your browser.

```
www.philoliver.com/visbasic/ControlsVBP.exe
```

This will download a self-extracting file to your hard disc, after asking you where you want to place it. Save it in a folder of its own and run the file to obtain the files.

# Control Buttons

 The Test Buttons routine shows a traffic light which changes from green to amber and then red when a command button is clicked.

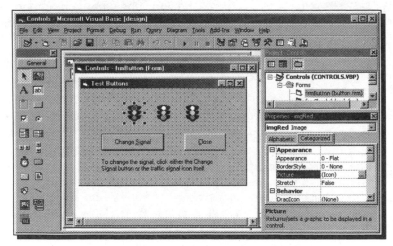

Fig. 8.4 Dissecting the Test Buttons Form

On close inspection, the form actually has three picture icons, with different colours active, superimposed on top of each other, with only one having its *Visible* property set as True. Clicking the **Change Signal** button calls the ChangeSignal procedure shown here.

```
Private Sub ChangeSignal()

    If imgGreen.Visible = True Then
        imgGreen.Visible = False
        imgYellow.Visible = True
    ElseIf imgYellow.Visible = True Then
        imgYellow.Visible = False
        imgRed.Visible = True
    Else
        imgRed.Visible = False
        imgGreen.Visible = True
    End If
End Sub
```

This steps through the colour sequence in the right order setting only one as *Visible* at a time.

Note that ChangeSignal is a Sub procedure not related to any particular object action (such as clicking the mouse). It can be called from anywhere on the current form and so is placed in the **(General)** procedure section.

Before we leave the Buttons part of the program, look at the code that is activated by clicking the **Close** button.

```
Unload Me
```

As its name suggests, this closes the active window and wipes its display from the screen. In this program, control then returns to the frmMain opening window.

## Check Boxes

 Check boxes are used on the WordWrap form which also gives a clear demonstration of how the *AutoSize* and *WordWrap* properties of a Label work.

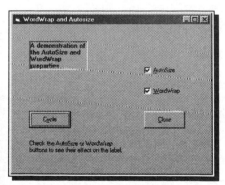

Fig. 8.5 The WordWrap Form

A long caption has been entered into a Label of specific size. Clicking the two check boxes selects whether the *AutoSize* and *WordWrap* properties of a Label are to be set or not.

When the program is run, you can change the check box settings and see the result immediately in the label. Clicking the **Cycle** button steps you through the different combinations of label properties, and the result can be seen in the display. The code behind the **Cycle** button is:

```
Private Sub cmdCycle_Click()
    ' cycle through the four possible combinations

    ' 1 Neither check box is selected
    If chkAutoSize.Value = 0 And _
     chkWordWrap.Value = 0 Then
        ' select the AutoSize check box
        chkAutoSize.Value = 1
    ' 2 Both check boxes are selected
    ElseIf chkAutoSize.Value = 1 And _
     chkWordWrap.Value = 1 Then
        ' deselect the AutoSize check box and
        ' select the WordWrap check box
        chkAutoSize.Value = 0
        chkWordWrap.Value = 1
    ' 3 Only the WordWrap check box is selected
    ElseIf chkAutoSize.Value = 0 And _
    chkWordWrap.Value = 1 Then
        ' deselect both check boxes
        chkAutoSize.Value = 0
        chkWordWrap.Value = 0
    ' 4 Only the AutoSize check box is selected
    Else
        ' select the WordWrap check box - the
        ' AutoSize check box is already selected
        chkWordWrap.Value = 1
    End If
End Sub
```

This routine checks and changes the AutoSize and WordWrap check box settings which themselves change the *AutoSize* and *WordWrap* settings of the label in the Display procedure on the **(General)** section of the form, as shown below. If either is selected, its *Value* property will be '1' and will set the Label property to 'True', as shown here.

```
If chkWordWrap.Value = 1 Then
    lblDisplay.WordWrap = True
End If
If chkAutoSize.Value = 1 Then
    lblDisplay.AutoSize = True
End If
```

A Check box displays an X when selected and, as we have seen, is used to give the user True/False or Yes/No options. They are usually used in groups to display multiple choices, any of which can be selected.

Check boxes and Option buttons function similarly but only one Option button in a group can be selected.

To display text next to the Check box, enter it into the *Caption* property of the box.

The *Value* property determines the state of a Check box, as used in the above program - the available settings being:

*0*   is Unchecked, the default setting.
*1*   is Checked, or selected.
*2*   is Greyed (dimmed), or unavailable.

# Option Buttons

An Option button displays an option that can be turned on or off. They are used to display multiple choices from which the user can select only one. You can group option buttons by drawing them inside a frame or a picture box, or directly onto a form. All those placed directly onto a form are treated as a separate group.

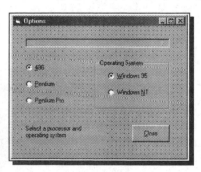

Fig. 8.6 The Options Form

The Options example, shown here, uses two groups of Option buttons, one in a frame and the other straight onto the form itself. The choice made in the left group of buttons sets a value to the string variable strComputer. That made in the right grouping sets a value to the variable strSystem.

The two default Options (in this case **486** and **W**indows 95), have their *Value* properties set to True, so they are 'selected' when the program is first run. At start-up the other Options will then have their *Value* properties as False.

In this example, when an Option is clicked, one of the two variables strComputer or strSystem is set, as shown in the procedure below.

```
Private Sub opt486_Click()
    ' assign a value to the first string variable
    strComputer = "486"
    ' call the subroutine
    Call DisplayCaption
End Sub
```

The DisplayCaption sub routine is then called, which builds up the message displayed in the Label field.

```
Sub DisplayCaption()
    ' concatenate the caption with the two string
    ' variables.
    lblDisplay.Caption = "You selected a " & _
      strComputer & " running " & strSystem
End Sub
```

# Combo and List Boxes

 These are both used to display a list of items from which the user can choose one. The list can be scrolled if it has more items than can be displayed at one time. A list box only allows a choice from an existing list, whereas a Combo box has a Text box feature at the top of the list, into which the user can type a new choice.

Dependant on the *Style* property, *Text* determines the text that is contained in the text edit area of a Combo box, or the selected item in the list box. This property is read-only at both design and run time.

The *Style* property sets the type of combo box drawn:

**0 - Dropdown Combo**    Includes a drop-down list and an edit area. The user can select from the list, or type into the edit area.

**1 - Simple Combo**    Includes an edit area and a list that is always displayed. The user can select from the list, or type into the edit area. By default, this type is sized so that none of the list shows. Increasing the *Height* property will show more of the list.

**2 - Dropdown List**    This style only allows selection from the drop-down list.

If the *Sorted* property is set to 'True', all items in a list are automatically alphabetically sorted at run time. The default setting, 'False', does not sort a list.

## A Simple Telephone List

The following small program shows how Combo, or List, boxes can be loaded at run time, and usefully used. It represents a very small telephone 'directory' with, as it stands, only room for 5 entries, but it could very easily be extended.

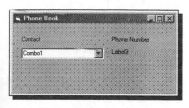

Fig. 8.7 Example32 Form

The form, shown here in Design mode, has a Combo box and three labels. The only reason a List box is not used is that it takes up much more room on the form!

Set the *Style* property of the Combo to the default **0 - Dropdown Combo** and the *label Caption* properties as shown in Fig. 8.7.

We will use two arrays, one to hold the names and the other, the telephone numbers, so place the following code in the General Declarations section of the form.

```
Dim SName(0 To 4)          ' Dimension arrays.
Dim TelNum(0 To 4)
```

The main body of the code loads the arrays with data and then places the names in the Combo list. This should be carried out when the program first starts up, so the code is placed as a Form_Load procedure.

```
Private Sub Form_Load ()              ' EXAMPLE32.MAK
    Dim I As Integer                  ' Declare variable.

' Enter data into arrays.
    SName(0) = "Jane Dean"
    SName(1) = "Leona Woolgatherer"
    SName(2) = "Angie Smith"
    SName(3) = "Sheila Splurg"
    SName(4) = "Joan Bloggs"
    TelNum(0) = "0173 789987"
    TelNum(1) = "54645"
    TelNum(2) = "010 45 678123"
    TelNum(3) = "01209 311887"
    TelNum(4) = "789456"

    For I = 0 To 4          ' Add names to list.
        Combo1.AddItem SName(I)
    Next I
    Combo1.ListIndex = 0   'Display first list item
End Sub
```

You could obviously substitute more meaningful data in the above if you wanted. All that remains now is to place a line of code behind the Combo so that the telephone number of the person selected in the List shows in the main Label box.

```
Private Sub Combo1_Click ()
    ' Display corresponding Number for name.
    Label3.Caption = TelNum(Combo1.ListIndex)
End Sub
```

When you have entered the code and are happy with the way it works, try changing the *Style* property of the Combo box to see the different types available. With the above code, whatever you do, don't try sorting the list with the *Sorted* property.

The array indices would not then be the same and incorrect phone numbers would be displayed!

As we saw in this previous example, to display items in a combo or list box, you use the **AddItem** statement. To remove items, you would use **RemoveItem** in the same way.

The *ListIndex* property determines the index of the currently selected item in a list; this cannot be used at design time. The *ListCount* property (also not available at design time) specifies the number of items in the list. The statement

```
Combo1.ListCount
```

would return the number of items in the list of Combo1.

# The Timer Control

Visual Basic's timer, which is invisible to the user at run time, is used for background processing. A Timer Control runs code at regular intervals by causing a Timer event, which occurs when a pre-set interval of time has elapsed. The timing frequency is set in the control's *Interval* property, which specifies the length of time in milliseconds. The other main Timer property is the *Enabled* property. When this is set to True with the *Interval* property greater than zero, the Timer event waits for the period specified in the *Interval* property.

A very simple digital clock can be programmed by placing a Timer and a Label on a form as shown on the left of Fig. 8.8. The clock running is shown on the right.

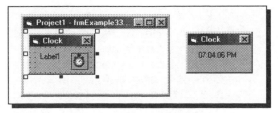

Fig. 8.8 A Simple Digital Clock

The code required is minimal, consisting of just two lines.

```
Private Sub Form_Load ()
    Timer1.Interval = 1000   ' Set timer interval.
End Sub

Private Sub Timer1_Timer ()
    Label1.Caption = Time   ' Update time display.
End Sub
```

In the first procedure, the Timer *Interval* property is set to 1000 milliseconds, or 1 second. In the second, the Timer is set to call the Visual Basic Time function after every 1 second interval, the Label *Caption* being updated every second with the computer system time.

As we saw, when run, a digital clock is operational in the window. By changing the form and label properties, and formatting the Time output (see Appendix C), you could customise this 'clock' with alarms, colours and fonts, etc.

# Pictures and Images

Visual Basic makes it easy to display and manipulate graphic images and pictures. They can be placed straight onto a form itself, or into Picture box and Image controls.

## Supported Graphic Formats

Visual Basic can display picture files in any of the following standard formats.

| *Format* | *Description* |
|---|---|
| Bitmap | A bitmap (with file name extensions **.bmp** or **.dib**) defines an image as a pattern of dots or pixels. You can use bitmaps of various colour depths, including 2, 4, 8, 16, 24, and 32 bits, but a bitmap only displays correctly if the display device supports the colour depth used by the bitmap. |

| | |
|---|---|
| Icon | An icon (with file name extension **.ico**) is a special kind of bitmap, with a maximum size of 32 pixels by 32 pixels. |
| Cursor | Cursors (with file name extension **.cur**), like icons, are essentially bitmaps, but they contain a 'hot spot', a pixel that tracks the location of the cursor by its x and y co-ordinates. |
| Metafile | A metafile is different as it defines an image as coded lines and shapes. Conventional metafiles have the file name extension **.wmf**, and enhanced metafiles **.emf**. |
| JPEG | JPEG (with file name extensions **.jpg** or **.jpeg**) is a compressed bitmap format which supports 8- and 24-bit colour. At 24-bit resolution it is an ideal format for photographs and is commonly used on the Internet. |
| GIF | GIF (with file name extension **.gif**) is a compressed bitmap format which was originally developed by CompuServe. It supports up to 256 colours and is also a popular file format on the Internet. |

## The Picture Box Control

The picture box control is similar to the Image control in that each can be used to display graphics in your application, but a picture box can act as a container for other controls and also supports graphics methods (such as Circle, Line, and Point), and text printing.

Pictures can be loaded into a Picture box control at design time by selecting them in the *Picture* property (in the Properties window), or at run time by using the *Picture* property and the LoadPicture function, as follows.

```
picMain.Picture = LoadPicture ("fred.jpg")
```

The LoadPicture function can actually have more settings for picture control and selection, but we will not get too involved here. Try the Help system if you ever need them.

To clear the graphic from the picture box control, use the LoadPicture function without specifying a file name.

By default, graphics are loaded into a Picture box at their original size, so if the graphic is larger than the control, the image will be clipped. You can make a picture box automatically resize to display an entire graphic by setting its *AutoSize* property to True. The control will then grow or shrink in size to that of the graphic, but be careful as this can lead to some interesting problems with large pictures. Unlike the Image control, however, the Picture box control cannot stretch the image to fit the size of the control.

To show how easy it is to add pictures, we will modify the phone book created in EXAMPLE32 to show the photo of the selected person, as well as their phone number. A modern 'little black book' maybe!

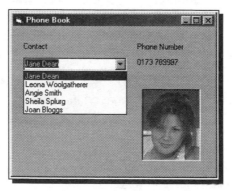

Fig. 8.9 A More Visual Phone Book

To do this, you add a Picture box to the form, as shown in Fig. 8.9 above, and set its *AutoSize* property to True. You must have photograph files of all your 'contacts' reduced to a suitable size for the form. In our example, these were scanned in as .jpg files which were saved in the same folder as the project itself.

We will use another array to hold the names of these graphic files, so add the following code in the General Declarations section of the form to dimension the array.

```
Dim Photo(0 To 4)
```

To load the pictures into the new array when the program starts, add the following code to the Form_Load procedure.

```
Photo(0) = "jane.jpg"
Photo(1) = "leona.jpg"
Photo(2) = "angie.jpg"
Photo(3) = "sheila.jpg"
Photo(4) = "joan.jpg"
```

If you prefer, you can keep the graphic files in another folder, but you then have to include the path to them in each of the above statements. All that remains to be done now is to add the following LoadPicture statement to the Combo1_Click() sub procedure:

```
' Display corresponding Picture for name.
picPhoto.Picture = LoadPicture(Photo(Combo1.ListIndex))
```

That's all there is to it. It is well worth doing this example. If you don't have any suitable graphic files to play with, ours are included in the Companion Disc.

## The Graphics Methods

Picture boxes and forms can be used to receive the output of the Visual Basic graphics methods such as Circle, Line, and Point. For example, you can use the Circle method to draw a circle in a picture box by setting the control's *AutoRedraw* property to True.

```
Picture1.AutoRedraw = True
Picture1.Circle (1200, 1000), 750
```

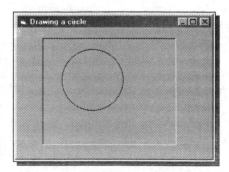

Fig. 8.10 A Circle in a Picture Box

Fig. 8.10 shows the result of running this code.

Setting *AutoRedraw* to True allows the output from these methods to be drawn to the control and automatically redrawn when the picture box control is re-sized or re-displayed after being hidden by another object.

## Drawing Lines

Perhaps the best way of demonstrating how easy it is to use the Line method in Visual Basic to draw freehand on a Form or Picture box is to create a small project.

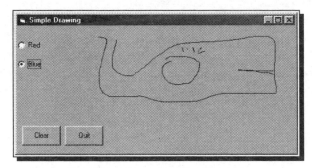

Fig. 8.11 A Simple Drawing Program

Fig. 8.11 shows our project at run time. Just one form (Form1) with the following controls on it with their respective properties:

| **Option1** | **Option2** |
|---|---|
| Name: optRed | Name: optBlue |
| Value: TRUE | Value: FALSE |
| Caption: Red | Caption: Blue |

| **Command1** | **Command2** |
|---|---|
| Name: cmdClear | Name: cmdExit |
| Caption:Clear | Caption: Exit |

When all four objects have been placed on the form, it's time to enter the source code. The two Command buttons are very simple. In cmdExit_Click, as usual, we just put **End** to exit the program. In cmdClear_Click, we put the following:

```
Form1.Cls
```

Cls (clear screen) simply clears the form when we are fed up with what is drawn.

Next double-click on the form to open the Code Editor, find the MouseDown Event of Form1 and type the following:

```
Form1.CurrentX = X
Form1.CurrentY = Y
```

This defines the X and Y co-ordinates when the mouse is clicked somewhere on the form at run time.

Lastly, put the following in the form's MouseMove Event:

```
Dim strColour As String

If optRed = True Then
    strColour = 4
End If

If optBlue = True Then
    strColour = 1
End If

If Button = 1 Then
Line (Form1.CurrentX, Form1.CurrentY)-(X, Y),_
QBColor(strColour)
End If
```

Now save the project as DRAWING.VBP and try it out. In this code we first declared the string strColour to represent the colour's numerical value to be used later in the QBColor function. Then two **If...Then** statements return the colour value of 4 (Red) if optRed is selected, or 1 (Blue) if optBlue is selected.

The last **If...Then** statement determines if the left mouse button is being pressed down on the form. If so, the program uses the Line method to draw a line as the user drags it across the form. QBColor is the colour which you program the line to be. Black would be 0 so you would write: QBColor = 0.

Overall, a line statement has the following form:

```
Line (X1, Y1) - (X2, Y2), QBColor(colour)
```

As usual with Visual Basic, it doesn't take much code to get some quite interesting results. Do try this example, you will find it well worth while. It could obviously be extended to include maybe, other colours, and line formatting features.

# Building a Menu Bar

To make creating menus for your windows reasonably easy, Visual Basic has a Menu Design window in which you can create custom menus and define their properties. Before we can demonstrate this procedure, though, you need a program with a form that needs a menu bar. We suggest you create the following small program.

## A Simple VAT Calculator

Appendix A contains all the code, complete with object properties, for you to build the small program named VATCALC.VBP, that asks for number input and then calculates and displays VAT information, as shown below.

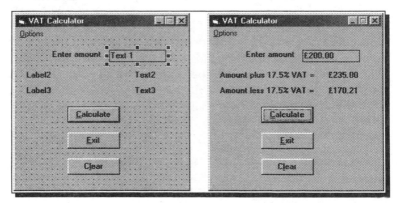

Fig. 8.12 The VatCalc Example in Design and Run Modes

The main form, **frmVatCalc** is shown on the left above in Design mode, and on the right in Run mode. The Label *Caption* and Text box *Text* properties are shown named above so that you can see where they are. These must all be deleted (in the Properties window) before the program will work properly!

You should have no problem building this form from what we have covered so far, except for the Menu bar. This has only one item (**Options**) on the main bar, and three sub-menu items when it is opened, as shown in Fig. 8.13.

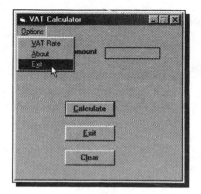

Fig. 8.13 The Opened Menu

Governments have a habit of increasing tax levels at regular intervals, so the first menu item allows the user to change the VAT rate (from the present 17.5%).

The **Exit** item is not really necessary, as this is already taken care of with a Command button, but it is always better to have too many ways out, than not enough.

The **About** menu item opens another form and displays some information about the program, as shown in Fig 8.14.

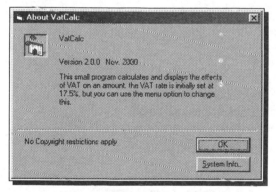

Fig. 8.14 A Standard Visual Basic About Dialogue Box

This is included to demonstrate some other techniques and was, in fact, almost 'automatically' created for us, because it is one of Visual Basic's standard forms that are available for you to use.

To create this form, click the Add Form toolbar button (see Fig. 7.5) and select the **Form** option. This opens the Add Form dialogue box shown in Fig. 8.15. Select About Dialog and click the **Open** button to add the standard form to your project. There are several other standard forms here, that are worth exploring.

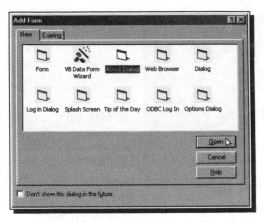

Fig. 8.15 The Add Form Dialogue Box

We will leave it to you to complete the About form. Have a look at the code already placed behind it. You will find that the Version and Application Title details are generated at run time from information placed in the **Project**, **Properties** dialogue box. The other text is placed at design time in the *Caption* properties of the Labels concerned.

## The Menu Design Window

With the main **frmVatCalc** form selected, choose **Menu Editor** from the **Tools** menu, or use <Ctrl+E>, or click the toolbar icon shown here. All of these will open the Menu Editor window, shown in Fig. 8.16.

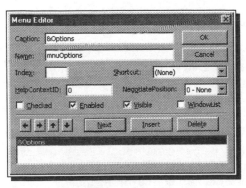

In the **Caption** text box, you type the menu item caption that you want displayed on the menu bar. In our case you type &Options.

The ampersand (&) character will give

Fig. 8.16 The Menu Editor

the user keyboard access to this menu item. At run time, the next letter is underlined, and the menu can be accessed by pressing **Alt** plus the access key, <**Alt+O**>.

If you had wanted to create a separator bar in your menu, you could type a single hyphen (-) in this box.

In the **Name** box, type the control name that will be used to refer to this menu item in code, in our case **mnuOption**.

Leave the other options in the Design Window at their default settings and click the **Next** button. Type **&VAT Rate** in the

**Caption** text box and **mnuVATRate** in the **Name** box. Now click the Right Arrow on the Window button bar to make this menu item secondary to the first, as shown here, and press **Next**. Add the other two menu items as follows:

| Caption | Name |
|---------|------|
| &About | mnuAbout |
| E&xit | mnuExit |

The Menu Design Window should now look like ours, shown below in Fig. 8.17. Pressing **OK** will close the window and place the menu bar on your form.

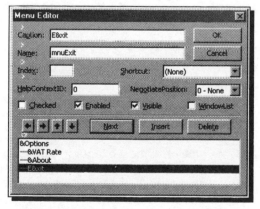

Fig. 8.17 The Completed Menu for VatCalc

Using the left and right arrows you can have up to four levels of sub-menus. The up and down arrows change the position of a menu item in the list box. We did not use the other features in the Design Window, but their functions are:

| | |
|---|---|
| **Index** | Type an index number to control the position of a menu item within a control array. |
| **Shortcut** | Use to assign a shortcut key to a menu item by selecting a key from the drop-down list. |
| **WindowList** | Select if you want the current menu control to include the name of open MDI child forms (outside the scope of this book). |
| **HelpContextID** | Enter a unique number if you plan to provide a context-sensitive Help topic. |
| **Checked** | Select if you want a check mark to appear at the left of a menu item to indicate that the control is turned on. |
| **Enabled** | Select if you want the menu item to initially respond to events. Clear the box if you want the menu item to be unavailable (greyed on the menu) to be enabled later in your code. |
| **Visible** | Select if you want the menu item to appear on the menu. |
| **NegotiatePosition** | Allows you to select the menu's NegotiatePosition property, which determines whether and how the menu appears in a container form. |

The menu items you created, although visible, will not do anything until you write code for them (as with other controls). In Design mode, if you click on a Menu Bar item the sub-menu will open, but if you click on a sub-menu item its code window will open. As an example, the code below is placed behind the **VAT Rate** sub-menu item.

```
Private Sub mnuVATRate_Click ()
' Get new VAT rate from user.
NVATRate = Val(InputBox$("Enter new VAT rate"))
VATRate = NVATRate
End Sub
```

This opens an Input Box that requires a new VAT rate to be entered. The other code for the two forms and all their controls is given in Appendix A.

The **Sub** mnuAbout_Click procedure loads the contents into the form named frmAbout with the statement

```
frmAbout.Show 1
```

The Show command displays a form. The following integer (1 or 0) sets the style as modal or modeless. When a form is modal, it must be removed with the **UnLoad** command before the program can continue. (Done in the **Sub** cmdAbout_Click procedure). The default is modeless, which lets the form stay active, and a 0 is not actually necessary.

# ActiveX Controls

An ActiveX control is an extension to the Visual Basic toolbox. They were formerly called OLE controls and are included with the Professional and Enterprise Editions of Visual Basic. ActiveX controls have the file name extension .ocx.

You use ActiveX controls just as you would any of the built-in intrinsic controls discussed so far. When you add one to a program, it becomes part of the development and run-time environment and adds new features to your application. For example, the Windows Common controls allow you to create applications containing 'Windows 95 type' toolbars, status bars, and directory structure tree views. Other controls allow you to create applications using the Internet.

With the above editions of Visual Basic, the setup procedure installs ActiveX controls automatically. You just add a control to your project Toolbox to use it in that project.

To do this, open the Components dialogue box with the
**Project**, **Components** menu command and you will find a list
of all the objects and ActiveX controls you can use. You just
select the check box to the left of a control name in the list, and
click on **OK**, to add it to the Toolbox.

## Some Provided Controls

The list below shows the main ActiveX controls provided by
Microsoft (MS). The ones you have on your system will depend
on the version of Visual Basic you are using.

| *Component Name* | *Control* |
|---|---|
| MS ADO Data Control 6.0 | ADO Data Control |
| MS Chart Control 5.5 | Microsoft Chart |
| MS Comm Control 6.0 | MSComm |
| MS Common Dialog Control 6.0 | CommonDialog |
| MS Data Bound Grid Control 5.0 | DBGrid |
| MS Data Bound List Controls 6.0 | DBList, DBCombo |
| MS Data Repeater Control 6.0 | DataRepeater |
| MS Data Grid Control 6.0 | DataGrid |
| MS Data List Controls 6.0 | DataList, DataCombo |
| MS FlexGrid Control 6.0 | MSFlexGrid |
| MS Grid Control | Grid |
| MS Hierarchical Flex Grid Control 6.0 | MSHFlexGrid |
| MS Internet Transfer Control 6.0 | Internet Transfer control |
| MS MAPI Controls6.0 | MAPIMessages, MAPISession |
| MS MaskedEdit Control 6.0 | MaskedEdit |
| MS Multimedia Control 6.0 | Multimedia MCI |
| MS PictureClip Control 6.0 | PictureClip |
| MS RemoteData Control 6.0 | RemoteData |
| MS RichTextBox Control 6.0 | RichTextBox |
| MS SysInfo Control 6.0 | SysInfo |
| MS TabbedDialog Control 6.0 | Microsoft Tab Control |
| MS Windows Common Controls 6.0 | TabStrip, Toolbar, StatusBar, ProgressBar, TreeView, ListView, ImageList, Slider, ImageCombo |
| MS Windows Common Controls-2 6.0 | Animation, UpDown, MonthView, DTPicker, FlatScrollbar |
| MS Windows Common Controls-3 6.0 | CoolBar |
| Ms Winsock Control 6.0 | WinSock |

# 9

## Functions and Procedures

## Standard Mathematical Functions

Visual Basic contains built-in functions to perform many mathematical operations. They allow calculations using such common functions as logarithms, square roots, sines of angles, and so on. As with earlier versions of BASIC, mathematical functions have a three-letter call name followed by a parenthesised argument. They are pre-defined and may be used anywhere in a program. Some of the most common standard functions are listed below.

### _____Standard Visual Basic Functions_____

| Name | Function |
|------|----------|
| **ABS**(X) | Returns the absolute value of X |
| **ATN**(X) | Arc-tangent of X (1.570796 to −1.570796) |
| **COS**(X) | Cosine of angle X, where X is in radians |
| **EXP**(X) | Raises e to the power of X |
| **INT**(X) | Returns the truncated integer part of X |
| **FIX**() | Returns the integer part of X |
| **LOG**(X) | Returns the natural logarithm of X |
| **SGN**(X) | Returns 1, 0 or −1 to reflect the sign of X |
| **SQR**(X) | Returns the square root of X |
| **SIN**(X) | Sine of angle X, where X is in radians |
| **TAN**(X) | Tangent of angle X, where X is in radians |
| **RND** | Generates a pseudo-random number from 0 to 1, but which does not include 1. |

Function calls can be used as expressions or elements of expressions wherever expressions are legal. The argument X of the function can be a constant, a variable, an expression or another function.

A more detailed explanation of using these functions is given below.

## ATN(X)

The arc-tangent function returns a value in radians, in the range +1.570796 to −1.570796 corresponding to the value of a tangent supplied as the argument X. Conversion from radians to degrees is achieved with the relationship Degrees = Radians*180/Pi, where Pi=3.141592654.

## SIN(X), COS(X) and TAN(X)

The sine, cosine and tangent functions require an argument angle expressed in radians. If the angle is stated in degrees, then use the relationship Radians = Degrees*Pi/180.

## SQR(X)

The **SQR** function returns the square root of the number X supplied to it.

To illustrate using some of the above functions, consider a simple problem involving a 2m-long ladder resting against a wall with the angle between ladder and ground being 60 degrees. With the help of simple trigonometry we can work out the vertical distance between the top of the ladder and the ground, the horizontal distance between the foot of the ladder and the wall and also the ratio of the vertical to horizontal distance.

The program uses the trigonometric functions **SIN, COS**, and **TAN**, to solve the problem.

```
Sub Form_Click ()      ' EXAMPLE36
                       ' Ladder against a wall
Dim AngleDeg, AngleRad, Vert, Horiz, RatioPi As Double
Dim Pi As Double
Pi = 3.141592654

AngleDeg = 60 'in degrees
AngleRad = AngleDeg * Pi / 180   ' In radians
Vert = 2 * Sin(AngleRad)
```

```
Horiz = 2 * Cos(AngleRad)
Ratio = Tan(AngleRad)

Print "Original angle = "; AngleDeg; Chr(176)
Print "Vert. distance = "; Format(Vert, "Fixed"); "m"
Print "Hor. distance = "; Format(Horiz, "Fixed"); "m"
Print "Ratio of Vert:Hor. = ";
Print Format(Ratio, "Fixed"); ":1"

End Sub
```

When the program is run and the opened window is clicked, Visual Basic will respond with

```
Original angle =   60°
Vert. distance =   1.73m
Hor. distance = 1.00m
Ratio of Vert:Hor. = 1.73:1
```

# ABS(X)

The **ABS** function returns the absolute (that is, positive) value of a given number. For example **ABS**(1.234) is 1.234, while **ABS**(−2.345) is returned as 2.345.

The **ABS** function can be used to detect whether the values of two variables say, X and Y, are within an acceptable limit by using the statement in the form

```
If Abs(X-Y) < 0.0001 Then
```

in which case the block of statements following the **THEN** will be executed only if the absolute difference of the two variables is less than the specified limit, indicating that they are approximately equal. We need to use the **ABS** function in the above statement otherwise a negative difference, no matter how small, would be less than the specified small positive number.

# EXP(X)

The exponential function raises the number e to the power of X. The **EXP** function is the inverse of the **LOG** function. The relationship is

```
Log (Exp (X)) = X
```

# LOG(X):

The logarithm to base e is given by the above function. Logarithms to the base e may easily be converted to any other base using the identity

```
log₀ (N) = LOG (N) /LOG (a)
```

where **log$_a$**(N) stands for the desired logarithm to base a, while **LOG**(N) and **LOG**(a) stand for the logarithm to the base e of N and a, respectively.

Antilogarithm functions are not provided but they can easily be derived using the following identities:

```
Antilog(X) = e^X    '(base e; this is Exp(X))
Antilog(X) = 10^X   '(base 10)
```

# INT(X) and FIX(X)

The integer functions returns the value of X rounded down to the nearest integer. Thus, **INT**(6.97) returns the value 6. The difference between **Int** and **Fix** is that if X is negative, **Int** returns the first negative integer less than or equal to X, but **Fix** returns the first negative integer greater than or equal to X. For example:

```
Int (-5.3) = -6
Fix (-5.3) = -5
```

**Fix**(X) is equivalent to:

```
Sgn (X) * Int (Abs (X))
```

Numbers can be rounded to the nearest whole number, rather than rounding down, by using the function **Int**(X+0.5). For example, **Int**(5.67+0.5) returns the value 6. It can also be used to round to any given number of decimal places, or to the nearest integer power of 10, by using the expression:

```
Int(X*10^D+0.5)/10^D
```

where D is (a) a positive integer or (b) a negative integer supplied by the user. For rounding to the first decimal, D=1; to the nearest 100, D=–2. The program below should help to illustrate these points.

```
Private Sub Form_Click ()        ' EXAMPLE37
                                 ' Rounding numbers
Dim X, N As Double
Dim D As Integer
Do
    X = Val(InputBox("Enter any number "))
    If X = 0 Then End
    D = Val(InputBox("Round to how many places?"))
    N = Int(X * 10 ^ D + .5) / 10 ^ D
    Print N
Loop Until False
End Sub
```

Try it yourself. To stop the program enter 0 (zero) in the first Input box, press its **X** close button, or the **Cancel** button.

## SGN(X)

The sign function returns 1 if X is positive, 0 if X=0, and –1 if X is negative.

## RND and RANDOMIZE n

The **Rnd** function is used to produce a pseudo randomly selected number from 0 to 1, but not including 1. The **Randomize** function allows the random-number generator **Rnd** to start from a 'seed number' and produce a series of numbers based on the seed. By using the same seed again, the same series of numbers can be obtained. The statement **Randomize**, by itself, uses the computer's internal clock to seed the random-number generator, while **Randomize n** seeds the random number generator **Rnd** with the number **n**.

Random numbers are used in statistical programs and in all kinds of simulations from simple games to complex computer models. In some programs, especially business simulations, it is necessary to reproduce the same 'random' conditions from run to run. This is done with the 'dice throwing' program given below. To see this, enter the following program.

```
Private Sub Form_Click () ' EXAMPLE38  -  Throwing dice
Dim I As Integer
    Randomize 2
    Print "THROW", "NUMBER"
    For I = 1 To 6
        Print I, Rnd
    Next I
End Sub
```

Every time it is run, the program produces the same random throws as shown below.

```
THROW          NUMBER
1              1.414126E-02
2              .6076428
3              .3568624
4              .9575312
5              .2980418
6              .7864588
```

In some contexts it is a severe disadvantage to have the same series of random numbers produced. You would then use the statement

**Randomize**

at the beginning of a program. When no seed number is given, this function uses the system clock to get its seed, and could be said to be 'truly random'.

In the previous dice throwing simulation the numbers were obviously not integers (as with dice). To produce random integers in a given range, use the formula:

**Int(** (Upper - Lower + 1) * **Rnd** + Lower)

where, Upper is the highest number in the range, and Lower is the lowest - for a dice these would be 6 and 1.

# Derived Mathematical Functions

For reference purposes, some useful mathematical functions which can be derived from standard Basic functions are listed below:

_____Derived Mathematical Functions_____

| *Function* | *Formula* |
|---|---|
| TRIGONOMETRIC | |
| Cosecant | CSC(X)=1/**SIN**(X) |
| Cotangent | COT(X)=1/**TAN**(X) |
| Secant | SEC(X)=1/**COS**(X) |
| | |
| INVERSE TRIGONOMETRIC | |
| Arc Cosecant | ACSC(X)=**ATN**(1/**SQR**(X*X-1))+(**SGN**(X)-1)*Pi/2 |
| Arc Cotangent | ACOT(X)=-**ATN**(X)+Pi/2 |
| Arc Secant | ASEC(X)=**ATN**(**SQR**(X*X-1))+(**SGN**(X)-1)*Pi/2 |
| | |
| HYPERBOLIC | |
| Hyp Cosine | COSH(X)=(**EXP**(X)+**EXP**(-X))/2 |
| Hyp Sine | SINH(X)=(**EXP**(X)-**EXP**(-X))/2 |
| Hyp Tangent | TANH(X)=-**EXP**(-X)/(**EXP**(X)+**EXP**(-X))*2+1 |
| Hyp Cosecant | CSCH(X)=2/(**EXP**(X)-**EXP**(-X)) |
| Hyp Cotangent | COTH(X)=**EXP**(-X)/(**EXP**(X)-**EXP**(-X))*2+1 |
| Hyp Secant | SECH(X)=2/(**EXP**(X)+**EXP**(-X)) |
| | |
| INVERSE HYPERBOLIC | |
| Arc Cosh | ACOSH(X)=**LOG**(X+**SQR**(X*X-1)) |
| Arc Sinh | ASINH(X)=**LOG**(X+**SQR**(X*X+1)) |
| Arc Tanh | ATANH(X)=**LOG**((1+X)/(1-X))/2 |
| Arc Cosech | ACSCH(X)=**LOG**((**SGN**(X)***SQR**(X*X+1)+1)/X) |
| Arc Cotanh | ACOTH(X)=**LOG**((X+1)/(X-1))/2 |
| Arc Sech | ASECH(X)=**LOG**((SQR(-X*X+1)+1)/X) |

**Note:** The constant Pi in the above formulae has the value of 3.141592654.

# User-Defined Function Procedures

In some programs it may be necessary to use the same mathematical expression in several places, and often using different data. User-defined functions enable definition of unique operations or expressions. These can then be called in the same manner as standard functions.

A user-defined function is defined as shown in the following example.

```
Function Area (Radius) As Double
    ' Calculates area of circle of Radius units
    Pi = 3.141592654
    Area = Pi * Radius ^ 2
End Function
```

Entering it into your program is made very easy; simply typing in an empty section of the Code Editor, the word **Function**, followed by its Name, will create a new code entry template for the function in the **(General)** section of the form, as shown here, in Fig. 9.1.

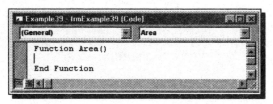

Fig. 9.1 A New Function Template, Ready to Enter Code

Enter the above function and the rest of this small program as shown below.

```
Private Sub Form_Click()    ' EXAMPLE39
    ' Using a user defined function
    Print "Radius", "Area of circle"
    For Radius = 1 To 10
        Print Radius, Area(Radius)
    Next
End Sub
```

You will also need to declare the variables used in the **(General) (Declarations)** section, like this:

```
Dim Radius, Pi As Double
```

The program calculates the areas of circles with radii of integer values between 1 and 10. The formula is given in the Function Area() statement and the Function is called the same way as Visual Basic's built-in functions. The value for the radius is passed to the function via a parenthesised variable which in fact could be any legal expression; its value is simply substituted for the function variable.

# The Object Browser

An easy way to track down the procedures and functions in your program is to use the Object Browser, which is opened with the toolbar icon shown here, or the **F2** key.

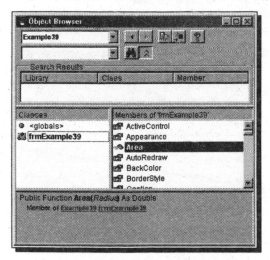

Fig. 9.2 The Object Browser

The Object Browser, as shown in Fig. 9.2, gives you details of all the procedures in your project, as well as the classes, properties, methods, events, and constants available from all the object libraries you have access to on your system.

You can use it to find and use objects you create, like the function in our example, as well as objects from other applications. You can get more information by searching for 'Object Browser' in the Help system.

# Sub Procedures

Visual Basic supports several kinds of procedures; user-defined Functions, Sub-procedures (or Subs), and Property procedures. The differences between them are that a Function returns a value, a Sub is complete in itself, and a Property procedure can return and assign values, and set references to objects.

Most of the Visual Basic code we have seen in this book so far has been made up of Event Procedures, or blocks of program code which are carried out when a certain action is implemented. You can also write your own Subs, which can then be called from anywhere in your program.

You enter a Sub into your program in the same way as described on the previous page for entering Functions (but you type Sub instead of Function). To illustrate how we can use a 'user defined' Sub-procedure, we will develop a small program which asks for the dimensions of three cylinders and calculates their volumes.

```
Private Sub Form_Click ()         ' EXAMPLE40
                                  ' Volume of 3 cylinders
Dim Radius As Double, Height As Double
Dim I As Integer
For I = 1 To 3
    Radius = Val(InputBox("Enter cylinder radius"))
    Height = Val(InputBox("Enter cylinder height"))
    Volume Radius, Height
Next I
End Sub
```

Here, the Volume statement is calling the following Sub, called Volume, and passing to it the values of Radius and Height.

```
Sub Volume (Rad As Double, Ht As Double)
    Dim BaseArea, Vol, Pi As Double
    Pi = 3.141592654
    BaseArea = Pi * Rad ^ 2
    Vol = BaseArea * Ht
Print "Cylinder radius = " & Rad & " units"
Print "Cylinder height = " & Ht & " units"
Print "Cylinder volume = " & Vol & " cubic units"
Print
End Sub
```

Note that the Sub above accepted the two arguments, even though they had different names. In older versions of Basic the Sub would have been called with the statement

```
Call Volume (Radius, Height)
```

This is acceptable to Visual Basic, but if used, the arguments must be enclosed in brackets, as shown. Just remember, no **Call**, no brackets!

After a Sub has been executed, program control is returned to the statement following the calling statement. It is, therefore, possible to build up a library of standard procedures, which can then be invoked from a main program to solve large and complex problems.

# Parameter Passing

There are two fundamental rules relating to parameter passing. These are: (a) the number of arguments in an argument list of the calling statement must be the same as that of the formal parameters, and (b) the data type of each argument must match the data type of the corresponding formal parameter.

The formal parameters in a procedure, whether a subprogram or function, are variable names local to that particular procedure. The actual parameter passed to the procedure can either be (i) a variable name local to the calling program or (ii) a literal, constant, or expression.

In the first case, when a parameter is a variable, parameter passing is by 'reference', which means that the address of the variable is passed to the procedure. As the formal parameter within the procedure is also assigned to the same address, this means that any changes to the formal parameter within the procedure can be passed back to the main program.

In the second case, when a parameter is a literal, constant, or an expression, parameter passing is by 'value', which means that the actual value is passed rather than the address in which the value is held. In this case, the value of an expression is calculated, the result is stored in a temporary location and the address of the temporary location is passed to the procedure. As a result, any change to this parameter by the procedure is only reflected in the temporary address and the original value accessed by the main program remains unmodified.

# Subroutines

Subroutines are similar to Sub procedures in many ways but they are not as powerful. They are supported by Visual Basic primarily for backward compatibility, so that programs written for standard BASIC can be easily adapted to run under Visual Basic.

## GOSUB and RETURN Statements

When Visual Basic encounters the **GOSUB** statement in the main body of the program, it branches to the first statement of the subroutine, and continues to execute the statements within the subroutine until the **RETURN** statement is encountered. This diverts program flow to the statement immediately following the **GOSUB** statement which called the subroutine. Thus, the **GOSUB** statement broadly corresponds to the **Sub** calling statement, while the **RETURN** corresponds to the **END SUB**.

When successive **GOSUB** statements branch to the same subroutine, each time the **RETURN** statement is reached, the main program is resumed at the last **GOSUB** statement from which it branched.

# 10

---

# Working with Files

Programs and 'data files' can be stored on disc quite easily and Visual Basic allows you to access them from your program front end with the standard Windows file handling dialogue boxes. Before describing this, though, we will spend some time getting to grips with some of the code needed to create and read from your own application data files.

Three types of data files can be used to store information, namely sequential, random access or binary files. Each type has advantages and disadvantages. Sequential files use disc space efficiently, but are difficult to update and best used for files which store only text. Random files are less efficient as far as usage of disc space is concerned, but provide quick access to information. Binary files offer great flexibility, but have no structure and, therefore, are difficult to program. We shall investigate the first two of these, by first looking at their individual structure and then by showing how data can be written to, and read from, each type of file.

---

## Sequential Data Files

A sequential data file can be thought of as a one dimensional array with each array location being one byte, capable of holding one character of a string. For example, the name of a friend together with his telephone number

```
ADAMS M. 02-1893
```

could be stored as shown below:

```
Byte                        1                   2
        0 1 2 3 4 5 6 7 8 9 0 1 2 3 4 5 6 7 8 9 0 1
Char    " A D A M S   M . " , " 0 2 - 1 8 9 3 " ¶ ⇓
```

---

Of special importance to sequential data files are the three ASCII control characters, 10 (linefeed – LF), 13 (carriage return – CR), together shown by the symbol ¶, and 26 (End-of-File marker – EOF), shown above as ⇓. The combination CR/LF (¶) is issued every time you press the <Enter> key.

Two names would be stored with details of the second following the first, separated by LF/CR, with the EOF character marking the end of the file. For example,

```
"ADAMS M.","02-1893"¶"SIMS I.","01-1351"¶⇓
```

Carriage return/linefeeds (¶) mark the end of blocks of information called 'records' with each record containing related information such as names and telephone numbers separated by commas, called 'fields'. Fields can hold any of the different types of variables, such as strings (which appear in quotation marks), integers, long integers, single- and/or double-precision variables.

To write data into a sequential data file you must write a small Visual Basic program which will 'create' such a file and then 'print' into it the characters representing the information you want to store on disc. To demonstrate this, we will develop the most simple ASCII text editor imaginable, which treats all the text in the file as one variable.

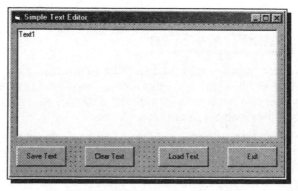

Fig. 10.1 Our 'Text Editor' in Design Mode

Open a new project and build the simple form shown in Fig. 10.1, which has one large Text box (Text1) and four command buttons, (cmdSave, cmdClear, cmdLoad, and cmdExit).

Make sure the *Multiline* property of the Text box is set to True, so that any long lines of text you enter will wrap onto subsequent lines, and that you clear the *Caption* property. Then enter the following code.

```
Dim Filename As String     ' General declaration

Private Sub cmdSave_Click ()        ' EXAMPLE41
 ' Save entered file to disc
 Filename = InputBox$("Enter file name")
 Open Filename For Output As #1
 Print #1, Text1.Text
 Close #1
End Sub

Private Sub cmdLoad_Click ()
 ' Load a text file from disc
 Filename = InputBox$("Enter file name")
 Open Filename For Input As #1
 Text1.Text = Input$(LOF(1), 1)
 Close #1
End Sub

Private Sub cmdClear_Click ()       ' Clear the text box
 Text1.Text = ""
 Text1.SetFocus
End Sub

Private Sub cmdExit_Click ()        ' Exit the program
 End
End Sub
```

To test out the program, run it, type a few lines of text into the editing section of the opened window and then save the text by clicking the **Save** button. To check that this worked, you could **Clear** the window and **Load** your file back again, or open your file into the Notebook. Even the Cut and Paste functions work (with their keyboard short-cuts), you can get a lot for a small amount of code with Visual Basic.

## Saving a File to Disc

In the cmdSave_Click Sub, following the InputBox line, the commands **Open** Filename **For Output As #**1, **Print** #1 and **Close** #1 are all directed to the filing system. The first opens the named file for output, through the communications channel #1. By opening a file, the name of that file is automatically written to the directory of the logged drive. If the filename already exists, the **Open** command will delete its contents, which means that you lose all the information already stored in that file. Once the data has been written to the file, with the **Print #** command, the file is **closed**.

Note the special way of writing Visual Basic commands which are directed to the filing system. They all end with the hash character (#), followed by the channel number n (with values between 1 and 255) through which you communicate with the file. Finally, when you finish with a file you close the communications channel with the **Close #**n command.

## Loading a File from Disc

Once your text file has been created, you must be in a position to read it back into the computer so that your information can be retrieved. This is done, in our example, with the short cmdLoad_Click procedure.

The third line **Open**s the file whose name is held in string variable Filename, for **Input** through channel #1. The next line reads the contents of the whole file using the **Input$** statement. The **LOF(1)** part of the statement gives the length of file to be input. Finally, the file is **Closed** as before.


As it stands, our text editor is usable but the file handling procedures, by Windows standards, leave a lot to be desired. You even have to remember the name of the file you want to retrieve! With one addition, however, and a few extra lines we can improve it enormously.

# The Common Dialogue Control

The Common Dialogue control, shown here, allows you to automatically use five of Windows' main dialogue boxes, and invoke the Windows Help System, from your programs. These are the Open, Save As, Print, Color and Font boxes. We will make use of the first two to improve our simple editor.

With Visual Basic 6.0 you must first add the Common Dialogue control to the Toolbox by selecting **Components** from the **Project** menu, locating and selecting the control in the Controls tabbed section, as shown in Fig. 10.2 below, and finally clicking the **OK** button.

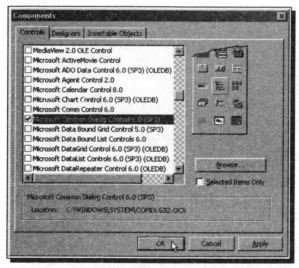

Fig. 10.2 Adding a Component to the Toolbox

A new icon, like that shown here, will be added to the Toolbox. In Design mode, drag a Common Dialogue control onto the form of the last example. It doesn't matter where you place it, as, like the Timer, it is invisible at run time. Then edit the code of the Save and Load procedures to that shown on the next page.

```
Dim Filename As String    ' General declaration
Dim F As Integer

Private Sub cmdLoad_Click ()
' Using OPEN dialogue box
CommonDialog1.Filter = "All Files (*.*)|*.*|Text _
Files (*.txt)|*.txt|Batch files (*.bat)|*.bat"
CommonDialog1.FilterIndex = 2
CommonDialog1.ShowOpen
Filename = CommonDialog1.Filename
F = FreeFile
Open Filename For Input As #F
Text1.Text = Input$(LOF(F), F)
Close #F
End Sub

Private Sub cmdSave_Click ()
' Using SAVE AS dialogue box
CommonDialog1.Filter = "All Files (*.*)|*.*|Text _
Files(*.txt)|*.txt|Batch files (*.bat)|*.bat"
CommonDialog1.FilterIndex = 2
CommonDialog1.ShowSave
Filename = CommonDialog1.Filename
F = FreeFile
Open Filename For Output As #F
Print #F, Text1.Text
Close #F
End Sub
```

The first extra line, in both cases, sets the *Filter* property to control what type of files will be displayed in the dialogue boxes. Each filter to be displayed needs a description and the actual filter, separated by the pipe character (|).

The line

```
CommonDialog1.ShowOpen
```

determines which Windows dialogue box is used. You use the appropriate method from the following table, to display one of the available dialogue boxes.

| Method | Dialogue box displayed |
|---|---|
| ShowOpen | Open |
| ShowSave | Save As |
| ShowColor | Color |
| ShowFont | Font |
| ShowPrinter | Print |
| ShowHelp | Invokes Windows Help |

In our example, the dialogue box returns the name of the file selected and stores it in the variable 'Filename' in the line

```
Filename = CommonDialog1.Filename
```

The screen dump in Fig. 10.3 shows our program, named EXAMPLE42.VBP, using the Save As dialogue box.

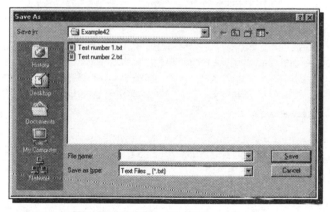

Fig. 10.3 The Save As Dialogue Box

You have probably noticed the line

```
F = FreeFile
```

in our modified code. As Visual Basic can access up to 255 file channels, it is safer and better practice, to use the **FreeFile** function to return the next file number available for use. If this is passed to a variable (F in our case), the variable can be used whenever a channel # is required.

## Trapping Errors

If you have not done it already, try pressing the **Cancel** button from one of the Common Dialogue boxes when your program is running. With the code given so far, Visual Basic stops the program running with the following message.

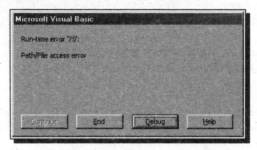

Fig. 10.4 A Run-time Error Message

The Open and Save As dialogue boxes handle most of the possible disc handling errors automatically (like having no disc in a drive), but it is left to you to handle what happens when the **Cancel** button is pressed. No real problem, just add the line

```
On Error GoTo ErrHandler
```

to the beginning of both the cmdLoad and cmdSave procedures, and add the following to their ends.

```
ErrHandler:
' User pressed Cancel button.
Exit Sub
```

# Random Access Files

Random-access data files are like a collection of equal-length sequential files, which means that each file can have a number of records (each with a record length specified by parameter **Len**). A visual representation of random access data files is shown below:

```
         1         2         3         4
12345678901234567890123456789012345678901234
--------------------------------------------
ADAMS M.             02-1893   iissssdddddddd
SMITH A. D.          03-864243 iissssdddddddd
LONGFELLOW A. B. C.  01-5513567iissssdddddddd
--------------------------------------------
```

In this example, each row represents a record and each record is divided into 5 'fields'. The first field, which is 20 characters long, contains names, the second, which is 10 characters long, contains phone numbers, the third to the fifth field contains numerical data which is encoded to strings of lengths 2, 4 and 8 characters, representing integer, single- and double-precision floating-point numbers, respectively. Thus the record length of each row in the above representation is 44 characters (20+10+2+4+8 = 44).

# Defining Records by TYPE

When using random access, Visual Basic requires you to define your records with the **Type**..**End Type** declaration. This allows the creation and storage of data in a composite format; mixing string and numeric types. A suitable **Type** definition for the above data would be:

```
Type Record
    Aname As String * 20
    Phone As String * 10
    Units As Integer
    Price As Single
    Amount As Double
End Type
```

To open a file and specify its length, with this data would require the following statement:

```
Open Filename For Random As #1 Len = 44
```

As random access is the default for the **Open** statement, the words **For Random** are not strictly required, but we recommend that you get used to including them.

The next program, EXAMPLE43.VBP, shows how data sets can be entered into a form and added to a random access file from the form. It is intended more as a demonstration than to perform a useful task, but the principles can be adapted to almost any kind of consistent format data entry.

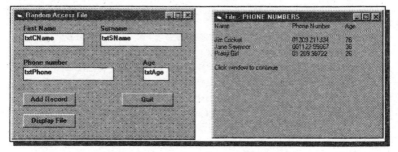

Fig. 10.5 A Random Access File Example

The main form layout is shown above on the left. It consists of four Text boxes to receive the data, each with a Label to identify it, and three Command buttons to control the entry or retrieval of data to and from a file.

Build this form, as shown, but don't forget to clear the *Text* properties of the Text boxes, as the names above are only to help identify them. Then open one more form and a module (see Fig. 7.5). The second form is used purely to receive printed output from the data file, as shown on the right above.

The module file, with the extension .BAS, is needed to hold the Type definition. Save all the files into a folder of their own, and enter the code shown on the next few pages.

This first code is placed in the separate module. It defines a custom data type 'Record'. The **Option Explicit** statement forces Visual Basic to accept only declared variables.

```
Option Explicit
Type Record
 FirstName As String * 20
 SurName  As String * 15
 Phone As String * 12
 Age As Integer
End Type
```

The next code is for Form1, the 6 **Dim** statements being placed in the general declarations section of the form.

```
Dim Person As Record
Dim RecordLen As Long
Dim F As Integer    ' Filenumber
Dim Msg As String
Dim FileName As String
Dim Position As Integer ' To track record number

Private Sub Form_Load ()
 ChDrive App.Path
 ChDir App.Path
 RecordLen = Len(Person)
 Msg = "Give file name for data"
 FileName = InputBox$(Msg)
 F = FreeFile
 Open FileName For Random As F Len = RecordLen
 Position = 1
End Sub

Private Sub cmdAddRecord_Click ()
 GetRecord              ' Load data from text boxes
 Put #F, Position, Person    'Save to file
 Position = Position + 1     'Increase pointer
 txtCName.Text = ""    ' Empty text boxes
 txtSName.Text = ""
 txtPhone.Text = ""
 txtAge.Text = ""
 txtCName.SetFocus
End Sub
```

```
Private Sub cmdDisplayFile_Click ()
Dim I As Integer, Caption As String
Caption = "File - " + UCase$(FileName)
Form2.Caption = Caption            ' Name window
Form2.Show                         ' Open a print window
Form2.Print "Name"; Tab(30); "Phone Number";
Form2.Print Tab(50); "Age"
Form2.Print
For I = 1 To Position - 1
    Get #F, I, Person    ' Read a record from file
    ' Trim blanks from and print the record
    Form2.Print Trim$(Person.FirstName);
    Form2.Print " " + Trim$(Person.SurName);
    Form2.Print Tab(30); Trim$(Person.Phone);
    Form2.Print  Tab(50); Trim(Person.Age)
Next I
Form2.Print
Form2.Print "Click window to continue"
End Sub

Sub cmdQuit_Click ()
Close #F                 ' Close the file
    Kill FileName        ' Delete file from disc
End
End Sub

Sub GetRecord ()
' Load PERSON variable from text boxes
Person.FirstName = txtCName.Text
Person.SurName = txtSName.Text
Person.Phone = txtPhone.Text
Person.Age = Val(txtAge.Text)
End Sub
```

The last code, below, is placed in the Click procedure of
Form2. This lets you remove the print window when you are
happy that your data file is working.

```
Sub Form_Click ()
    Form1.txtCName.SetFocus
    Unload Me
End Sub
```

The random access method only works if, after declaring a data Type, you then declare a variable of that type, as done in the line

```
Dim Person As Record
```

The Form_Load Sub is actioned when Form1 is opened at run time. The **ChDrive** and **ChDir** statements set the current drive and directory to that of the running application. This is so that the location of the file created is controlled. The line

```
RecordLen = Len(Person)
```

passes the length of our defined data Type to a variable, which is then used in the **Open** statement.

You are then expected to enter data manually into the text boxes. When happy with your data, click the **Add Record** button which actions the cmdAddRecord Sub.

This, first calls the Sub 'GetRecord' which loads the data elements from the text boxes to the respective components of the 'Person' variable. It then **Put**s this data, as one record, into the previously opened file

```
Put #F, Position, Person
```

F represents the channel number used to communicate with the opened file. The 'Position' variable keeps track of the record number being processed, and is incremented after the **Put** operation. The text boxes are then emptied and the focus returned to the first one, so that you can continue to add as many records as you want.

When you want to view all the records entered, click the **Display File** button which activates the cmdDisplayFile Sub. This sets the caption of Form2 and opens it with the **Show** command. The **Get** statement is used to retrieve the data from the file, one record at a time.

```
Get #F, I, Person
```

It is the complement of the **Put** statement. Each record is then **Trim**med, to remove any padding spaces, and printed to the opened Form2 window.

When you have worked out how it all functions, you can press the **Quit** button, which **Close**s the open file and deletes it from your disc with the **Kill** statement. In a working application you would not need this line, but we have added it to save your hard disc getting cluttered.

We have tried to make the code of these examples as simple as possible, to make them easier to understand, so there is little attempt at error trapping or other sophistications.

If you want to develop the programs further, we suggest you first study the sample programs provided with Visual Basic.

# Binary Files

A binary file is the most rudimentary type of file which offers the greatest flexibility, but its use imposes considerable responsibility on the programmer as binary files do not have any structure. They are a sequence of characters without any delimiters, or records. The characters simply occupy positions 0, 1, 2, and so on, within the file. They are used when you need to keep the size of your data files to the absolute minimum.

Due to their complexity we will not give any more detail on binary files here, as they are a little outside the scope of this book.

# Drive, Dir and File List Boxes

   There are also three controls included on the standard Visual Basic Toolbox that allow you to easily list drives, folders and files. We must say a few words on these before leaving the subject of files, but you may find that the Common Dialogue features are really all you need. Try putting one of each of these onto an empty form, as shown in Fig. 10.6.

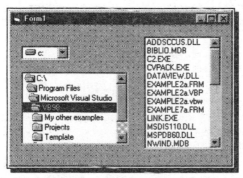

Fig. 10.6 The DriveList, DirList and FileList Box Controls

When placed they access your system as shown, and if you run the form as it is, each box will access your drives, folders and files. You must place code, though, to link the boxes together so that the files shown represent those of the folder selected, for example.

The DriveList control has a *Drive* property which uses the following syntax:

```
Drive1.Drive = Drive
```

The DirList and FileList controls have a *Path* property which uses the following syntax:

```
File1.Path = Path
Dir1.Path = Path
```

It is very easy to write code to link the three controls. With the following code, when you change the drive, or folder, the other lists are updated.

```
Private Sub Drive1_Change()              ' EXAMPLE44
    On Error GoTo DriveHandler
    ' Update directory list box to synchronise with the
    ' drive list box.
    Dir1.Path = Drive1.Drive
    Exit Sub
' If there is an error, reset Drive1.Drive with the
' drive from Dir1.Path.

DriveHandler:
    Drive1.Drive = Dir1.Path
    Exit Sub
End Sub

' This event occurs when a new directory is selected
Private Sub Dir1_Change()
    ' Update file list box to synchronise with the
    ' directory list box.
    File1.Path = Dir1.Path

End Sub
```

As you can see, this requires very little code. There is even an error trapping routine to cope with the time that the user selects a removable drive with no disc in it. Without this the program would just stop.

In our routine above, to actually use the results of the file selection procedure in more code, you would use **File1.FileName** to represent the name, and **Dir1.Path** to represent the path of the selected file.

You can use the Drive property to change drives at the operating system level by specifying it as an argument to the ChDrive statement, such as:

```
ChDrive Drive1.Drive
```

To set the current working directory, use the ChDir statement. For example, the following statement changes the current directory to the one displayed in the directory list box:

```
ChDir Dir1.Path
```

## An Image Viewer

Before we leave this section, we will give an example of how these features could be used to create a simple, but useful, image viewer. For this, you can use the previous EXAMPLE44.VBP form and code, but with the Drive, Directory and File List Boxes re-arranged as shown in Fig. 10.7.

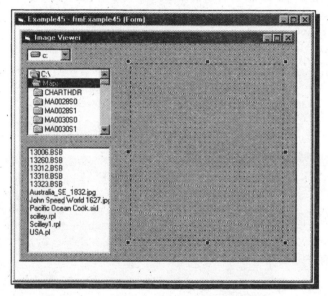

Fig. 10.7 The Design Form for an Image Viewer

One more thing, before the form is complete, is to drag an Image Control from the Toolbox, as shown above. Give this control the *Name* property imgGraphic, but leave the other properties with their default settings.

Now for the code. Double-click on the form in Design mode to open the Code Editor and add the following procedure.

```
Private Sub Form_Load()
Filel.Pattern = "*.jpg; *.gif"
End Sub
```

This is actioned when the form is loaded and filters the contents of the File List Box to display only .jpg and .gif graphic files.

In the Sub Dir1_Change add the lines

```
ChDrive Drive1.Drive
ChDir Dir1.Path
```

These set the selected drive and folder, or directory, as the current system ones. Any files then selected will not need to be given a path. Then add one more procedure, as follows:

```
Private Sub File1_Click()
imgGraphic.Picture = LoadPicture(File1.FileName)
End Sub
```

This simply uses the LoadPicture function (see page 143) to load the selected graphic file into the Image control when the File List is clicked. You could also use **Set** to do this:

```
Set imgGraphic.Picture = LoadPicture(File1.FileName)
```

Fig. 10.8 The Image Viewer in Operation

Give it a try. When you run this example you can have a quick look at all the graphic files you have filled your hard disc with. We have actually produced something useful, at last!

# 11

# Working with Other Applications

The fact that Microsoft's Office applications, Word, Access and Excel, use Visual Basic themselves makes it easy to interact with them. As the majority of developed programs have to process data of some kind, perhaps the most important link is that between databases and Visual Basic itself.

## The Data Control

The Data control, shown here, is an intrinsic control located on the Toolbox that makes it very easy to create a database, as well as view and modify the data stored in many types of existing databases, including Microsoft Access, Btrieve, dBASE, Microsoft FoxPro, and Paradox. You can also use it to access Microsoft Excel, Lotus 1-2-3, and standard ASCII text files as if they were true databases. Visual Basic also includes the even more powerful ADO Data control (ActiveX Data Objects), but we will leave that one for you to explore.

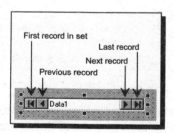

Fig. 11.1 A Data Control at Design Time

As shown in Fig. 11.1 above, the control has four buttons that allow the user to scroll backwards and forwards through the record set that is linked to it.

You don't need to have the Access program itself on your PC to work with its database files. In our next example, we will work with NWIND.MDB, one of the database files which should have been placed in the same folder as the Visual Basic program when it was installed, (see Fig. 1.6 for our details). If it is not there and you want to work through this, you will have to add it by re-running the Visual Basic Setup, as described on page 5.

Open a new project and add a Data control to it, as well as three labelled text Boxes as shown in Fig. 11.2.

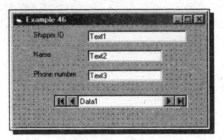

Fig. 11.2 Using a Data Control

The first thing to do is to connect the Data control to the database. With the Data control selected, find the *DatabaseName* property in the Properties Window, click the ▓ button in the right-hand side, and select the file NWIND.MDB.

Fig. 11.3 Properties

Next, select the *RecordSource* property and choose the Shippers table, as shown in Fig. 11.3, from the list of available tables in the database.

## Binding Controls

We have now 'locked' the Data control onto the table in the database we want, but we must set the Text boxes up so that they display the data in the table. This is called 'binding' the controls to the data source.

Make sure you delete the *Captions* of the Text boxes, and then set the *DataSource* property of each to the Data1 control. Next, set the *DataField* properties of each Text box to

ShipperID, CompanyName and Phone, for Text1, Text2 and Text3, respectively.

When you run the project, it should show the contents of one field of the database table and let you move easily between the other fields with the Data control buttons, as in Fig. 11.4.

Fig. 11.4 Using a Data Control

So, with no code at all, you can include a database viewer in your project; but by adding a few command buttons and using the code in the table below in their Click procedures you could do all your database editing, etc., from your project. Have another look at the code example on page 128, it should make more sense now! Good luck.

| Action | Code Needed |
|---|---|
| Add a Record | `Data1.recordset.addnew` |
| Delete a record | `Data1.recordset.delete`<br>`Data1.recordset.movenext` |
| Save changes | `Data1.recordset.update` |
| Move to next record | `Data1.recordset.movenext` |
| Edit a record | `Data1.recordset.edit` |
| Address a field | `Data1.recordset.fields("fieldname")` |
| Bookmark a record | `Let varX = Data1.recordset.bookmark` |
| Table record count | `Data1.recordset.count` |

# Visual Basic for Applications

As mentioned in the first chapter, VBA (Visual Basic for Applications) is included with the later versions of Microsoft Office. With this you can automate application procedures, or even develop customised applications of your own.

To access the feature from Word, Access or Excel, you use the **Tools**, **Macro**, **Visual Basic Editor** menu commands, or the <Alt+F11> keyboard shortcut. Fig. 11.5 below, shows the editor and some of its features opened from Word 2000.

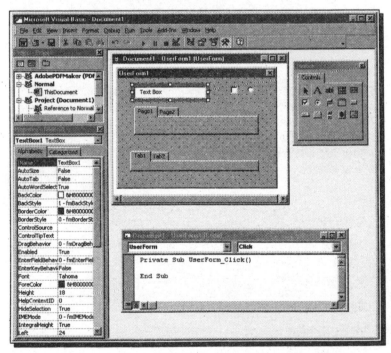

Fig. 11.5 The Visual Basic Editor Opened from Word 2000

Some of the features are very slightly different as they are designed to complement the Office applications, but on the whole VBA is the same as the standard Visual Basic 6.0 we cover in the rest of the book. If you are going down this route, it may be worth your while working through VBA's Help pages.

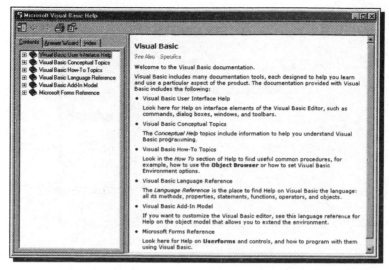

Fig. 11.6 Visual Basic for Applications Help Opening Page

As you would expect, these are accessed from the **Help** menu of whatever Office application Visual Basic Editor you are using.

# Connecting to Office Applications

It is possible to get Visual Basic to talk to and control both Microsoft Word and Excel with code, but the office applications need to be installed on the target machine before their objects can be accessed. They cannot be distributed with the application you create.

To assign the Application to an object variable, as we do here, the relevant object libraries have to be selected. To do this, use the **Project**, **References** menu command from Visual Basic 6.0 and select 'Microsoft Excel 9.0 Object Library' for Excel, and 'Microsoft Word 9.0 Object Library' for Word, as shown in Fig. 11.7. These are the library names for Office 2000 versions of Excel and Word. You may have different versions, in which case the names will not be the same, but you should be able to recognise what libraries to include.

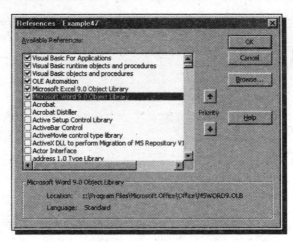

Fig. 11.7 Including the Word and Excel Object Libraries

## Working with Excel

Here is a small example showing how to connect to and talk with the Excel spreadsheet application.

```
Option Explicit
Dim xlsApp As Excel.Application

Private Sub Command1_Click()              'EXAMPLE47
    Set xlsApp = Excel.Application
    With xlsApp
        'Show Excel
        .Visible = True
        'Create a new workbook
        .Workbooks.Add
        'Put text in to the cell that is selected
        .ActiveCell.Value = "Hello there"
        ' Put text into cell A3 regardless of the
        ' selected cell
        .Range("A3").Value = "This is an example of _
        connecting to Excel"
    End With
End Sub
```

In this routine we put the object in the variable xlsApp and make Excel visible to the user. When Excel is started like this it does not contain a workbook, so one has to be created or opened. In this example we created a new workbook. Once there is a workbook open you can use it however you want in real time.

When you have finished with Excel, you can close it from Visual Basic as follows:

```
Private Sub Command2_Click()
    ' Close the workbook
    xlsApp.Workbooks.Close
    ' Close Excel
    xlsApp.Quit
End Sub
```

This routine first closes the workbook (if necessary bringing up a prompt from Excel asking if you want to save it), then closes Excel itself.

## Working with Word

The following routines work in a similar way with the Word word processor

```
Option Explicit
Dim wrdApp As Word.Application

Private Sub Command1_Click()          'EXAMPLE48
  Set wrdApp = New Word.Application
  With wrdApp
    'Show Word
    .Visible = True
    'Create New Document
    .Documents.Add
    'Add text to the document
    .ActiveDocument.Content.Text = "Hello there"
  End With
End Sub
```

The routine to close the document and application is:

```
Private Sub Command2_Click()
     'Close the current document
     wrdApp.ActiveDocument.Close
     'Close Word
     wrdApp.Quit
End Sub
```

As before, Word prompts you to save the document if it is necessary, before it will close down.

# 12

---

# Some Loose Ends

---

## Debugging Your Programs

As you develop more and more complicated code in your programs you will inevitably make mistakes and produce error messages. There are three types of errors you may encounter as you develop your applications.

### Compile Errors

These occur when your code is incorrectly constructed, such as a **Next** statement without a corresponding **For** statement, or a misspelled word, or a data type mismatch with your variables. Compile errors include syntax errors, which are errors in grammar or punctuation recognised by Visual Basic and are flagged by the compiler as you attempt to enter the code.

### Run-time Errors

These occur when you attempt to run your program. Common examples include attempting to write to a file that doesn't exist, or dividing by zero.

### Logical Errors

Often the most difficult type of error to correct is when the program doesn't perform as you expect, and produces incorrect results, because your programming logic is at fault.

The first of these error types are sorted out with the help of the compiler when you enter your code into the editor. Run-time and logic errors though, may need the help of Visual Basic's debugging tools, which let you look at the state of the program and all the variables, etc., in the middle of a run.

---

# Break Mode

So far we have encountered two of Visual Basic's operating modes. Design, when you enter controls and code, and Run when you start it running. There is a third one, Break mode, which is used for most of the debugging processes. You can easily see what mode you are currently in, as it is displayed on the title bar in brackets, as shown in Fig. 12.1.

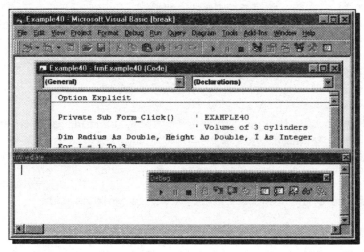

Fig. 12.1 A Program in Break Mode, with a Debug Toolbar

Any time a program is running you can change to Break mode by clicking the **Break** icon on the Toolbar, shown here. While in Break mode, the Immediate pane is opened and you can edit and debug your code and usually continue execution of the program.

# The Debug Tools

The best way to get a rapid overview of the debugging possibilities of Visual Basic is to spend ten minutes with the Help system. To do this, use the **Help**, **Index** menu command and search for 'debugging, basic concepts'.

Work your way through the presented screens which have been very professionally put together and show several working examples of debugging in practice.

## The Debug Toolbar

Most of the debugging tools are best accessed from the Debug toolbar. This is not open by default, but with the **View**, **Toolbars**, **Debug** toggle command.

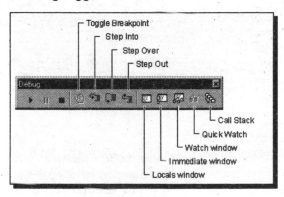

Fig. 12.2 The Debug Toolbar Icons

The icons on the Debug Toolbar have the following purposes:

| Debugging tool | Purpose |
|---|---|
| Breakpoint | Defines a line in the Code window where Visual Basic suspends execution of the application. |
| Step Into | Executes the next executable line of code in the application and steps into procedures. |
| Step Over | Executes the next executable line of code in the application without stepping into procedures. |
| Step Out | Executes the remainder of the current procedure and breaks at the next line in the calling procedure. |

| | |
|---|---|
| Locals Window | Displays the current value of local variables. |
| Immediate Window | Allows you to execute code or query values while the application is in Break mode. |
| Watch window | Displays the values of selected expressions. |
| Quick Watch | Lists the current value of an expression while the application is in Break mode. |
| Call Stack | While in Break mode, presents a dialogue box that shows all procedures that have been called but not yet run to completion. |

## Breakpoints

You can set breakpoints in your code in Design mode to halt your program execution at those points and check the values of variables or see what actions will be taken next.

To set a breakpoint, place the insertion point anywhere in a line of code where you want the program to stop and use the **Debug**, **Toggle Breakpoint** command, the **F9** function key, or click the **Toggle Breakpoint** icon on the Debug toolbar. Visual Basic adds the breakpoint and highlights the line.

## Using the Immediate Window

To execute code in the Immediate, or Debug window as it used to be called, **while in Break mode** you simply type a line of code in the window and press <Enter> to execute the statement.

In the Immediate window, you can do most of the things you do in the Code window, but statements in the Immediate window are not saved with the project.

# The Application Wizard

So far, all the examples in this book have been started either by changing an existing project, or 'starting from scratch'. There is an alternative in Visual Basic 6.0, and that is to build the framework of a new project semi-automatically using a wizard. As you probably know, a wizard in Microsoft terminology, is just an automated procedure.

To have a look at this feature, start Visual Basic but in the New Project dialogue box (see Fig. 2.2 on page 12) select the VB Application Wizard option, and click the **Open** button.

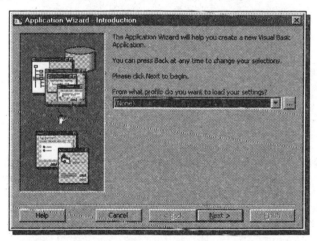

Fig. 12.3 The Application Wizard Opening Page

You move from page to page with the **Next** and **Back** buttons. Press the **Help** button if you don't understand anything on a page. The help information provided is very good.

This wizard really makes it easy to generate different types of very high quality programs which can contain a menu system, toolbar and a status bar. The default forms toolbar is similar to a Microsoft Office toolbar, and includes the **New, Open, Save, Print, Cut, Copy, Paste, Bold, Italic, Underline, Align Left, Align Right**, and **Centre** buttons. Explorer-style applications have a default toolbar with the Navigation Buttons, **Cut, Copy,**

**Paste**, **Delete**, **Properties**, **View Large Icon**, **View Small Icon**, **View List**, and **View Details** buttons. The status bar includes information about the status of the application and the date and time, as shown on our example form in Fig. 12.4.

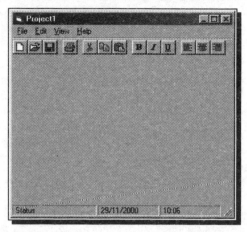

Fig. 12.4 A Form Generated with the Default Settings

Your application can contain a variety of different form types, many of which are way beyond our present scope. Once the application has been created, you have to modify the forms and controls to your exact needs. Many features will need code adding to them to make them actually do anything useful. To help here, the wizard adds "ToDo" notes in the comments where you need to customise the code, as shown below.

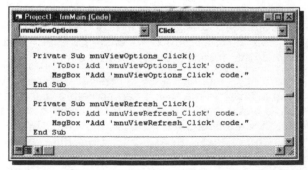

Fig. 12.5 Wizard Generated Code with "ToDo" Comments

# Compiling and Distributing

So far all the projects we have created have been run in the Visual Basic environment to test how they perform. That's fine during the development stage, but once your program is complete, you don't want to have to open Visual Basic every time you want to run the program.

At this stage you can compile the program code and create a .exe file from it. It then becomes an executable file which you can double click to make it run. This is easily done, as long as your project runs successfully. With the project open in Visual Basic, action the **File, Make ..... .exe** command. This will open the Make Project box for you to select a file name and destination. You can also click the **Options** button and add information about the program that will be included with its properties, as shown in Fig. 12.6.

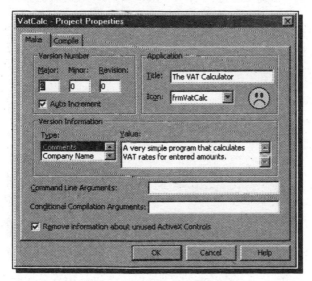

Fig. 12.6 Setting a Project's Properties

Your project will then be compiled and the executable file will be placed with the other project files, unless you specified an alternative location.

## Packaging

Compiling a project is fine as far as it goes, but the .exe file produced will only work on your PC, or on one that has all the library files on it that were used to create the program in Visual Basic.

To prepare a project so that it can be distributed on discs (or on the Internet) and installed and run on other PCs, there are two more stages to go through. In Microsoft speak, these are packaging and deployment and are carried out by the Visual Basic Package and Deployment Wizard.

You must first compile your project and create its .exe file. Then close Visual Basic and select Package and Deployment Wizard from the Visual Basic section of the Windows Start menu system to start the wizard, as shown in Fig. 12.7.

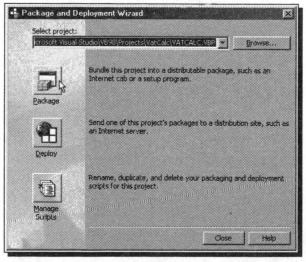

Fig. 12.7 The Main Screen of the Package and Deployment Wizard

Click the **Package** button and work your way through the series of screens that prompt you for information about your project and let you choose options for the package. Each screen explains what information is necessary before you can move on. For more information on any screen, press **F1** or click the **Help** button.

The wizard brings together all the files necessary for your project to run, and then packages them into .cab compressed files ready to place on the final distribution discs. Even for our tiny VATCALC example there were six files needed, five of which are shown below. The other was SETUP.EXE.

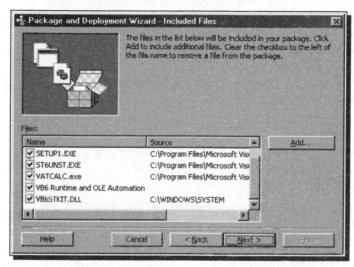

Fig. 12.8 The Files Included in the VATCALC Example

When the packaging operation is complete you will be presented with a report, maybe like ours shown next.

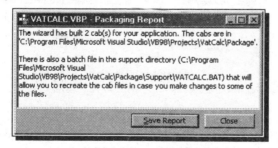

Fig. 12.9 A Packaging Report

## Deployment

The next stage is to click the **Deploy** button on the main wizard screen (see Fig. 12.7). This steps you through the procedure of loading the project's packaged files onto the disc or Internet media you specify. It took two 1.44MB floppy discs to hold the VATCALC package! I guess these days everything is geared to CD-ROMs.

The results from this whole procedure are excellent though. When the SETUP.EXE file produced is run, the package is very professionally installed onto your PC. Now we know where the dark blue installation screen came from.

The program is added to the Start menu system, as shown in Fig. 12.10 below, and is also added to the menu in the Add/Remove Programs 'applet' contained in the Control Panel. We hope all these features work with your version of Visual Basic, as they did with ours.

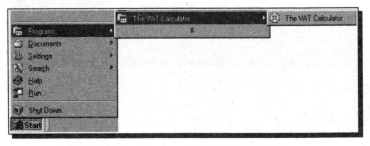

Fig. 12.10 Our Program Added to the Start Menu

\*\*\*\*\*\*\*\*\*\*\*\*\*\*\*\*\*\*\*\*

Well that's it folks. All that remains is a glossary and a range of Appendices with (hopefully) useful reference information to help with your Visual Basic programming. We have barely scratched the surface, but you should now be able to develop into those areas we could not mention.

# 13

# Glossary of Terms

| | |
|---|---|
| Access key | A key pressed while holding down the Alt key that allows the user to open a menu, carry out a command, select an object, or move to an object. For example, <Alt+F> opens the File menu. |
| Action query | A query that copies or changes data. |
| Active document | An ActiveX document or a document that contains ActiveX controls, Java Applets, or VBScript. |
| Active window | In an application, the window that appears in the foreground with a highlighted title bar or border to distinguish it from other visible windows. |
| ActiveX | Microsoft's brand name for the technologies that enable interoperability using the Component Object Model (COM). |
| ActiveX control | An object that you place on a form to enable or enhance a user's interaction with an application. ActiveX controls have events and can be incorporated into other controls. These controls have an .ocx file name extension. |
| Add-in | A customised tool that adds capabilities to the Visual Basic development environment. |
| Address | A unique number or name that identifies a specific computer or user on a network. |

| | |
|---|---|
| Alias | In Visual Basic, an alternate name you give to an external procedure to avoid conflict with a Visual Basic keyword, global variable, constant, or a name not allowed by the standard naming conventions. |
| ANSI Character Set | American National Standards Institute (ANSI) 8-bit character set used to represent up to 256 characters (0 – 255) using your keyboard. |
| API | Application programming interface. The set of commands that an application uses to request and carry out lower-level services performed by a computer's operating system. |
| Application | Software (program) designed to carry out certain activity, such as word processing, or data management. |
| Applet | A program that can be downloaded over a network and launched on the user's computer. |
| Archie | Archie is an Internet service that allows you to locate files that can be downloaded via FTP. |
| Argument | A constant, variable, or expression that supplies additional information to an action, procedure, or method. |
| Array | A set of sequentially indexed elements having the same intrinsic data type. Each element of an array has a unique identifying index number. |
| ASCII character set | American Standard Code for Information Interchange (ASCII) 7-bit character set widely used to represent letters and symbols found on a standard U.S. keyboard. |

ASP
Active Server Page. File format used for dynamic Web pages that get their data from a server based database.

Assignment statement
A statement that assigns a value to a variable or property. A Set statement assigns an object reference.

Automation
A technology that enables applications to provide objects in a consistent way to other applications, development tools, and macro languages.

AVI
Audio Video Interleaved. A Windows multimedia file format for sound and moving pictures.

Backbone
The main transmission lines of the Internet, running at over 45Mbps.

Backup
To make a back-up copy of a file or a disc for safekeeping.

Bandwidth
The range of transmission frequencies a network can use. The greater the bandwidth the more information that can be transferred over a network.

Benchmark
A type of test used to measure hardware and software performance.

Binary format
Machine-readable form. This format is different from ASCII or ANSI formats, which encode data as text.

Bit
A binary digit; the smallest unit of data a computer can store. Bits are expressed as 1 or 0.

Bitmap
An image represented by pixels and stored as a collection of bits in which each bit corresponds to one pixel. On colour systems, more than one bit corresponds to each pixel. A bitmap usually has a .bmp file name extension.

| | |
|---|---|
| Bookmark | For the Internet, a saved reference (in the form of a URL or hyperlink) to a particular location, page, or site, making it easy to return there. |
| Boolean data type | A data type with only two possible values, True (–1) or False (0). Boolean variables are stored as 16-bit (2-byte) numbers. |
| Boolean expression | An expression that evaluates to either True or False. |
| Bound control | A data-aware control that can provide access to a specific column or columns in a data source through a Data control. |
| Break mode | Temporary suspension of program execution in the development environment. In break mode, you can examine, debug, reset, step through, or continue program execution. |
| Breakpoint | A selected program line at which execution automatically stops. |
| Browser | Software that interprets HTML, formats it into Web pages, and displays it to the user. Modern browsers can also contain ActiveX components and can play sound or video files. |
| Buffer | A temporary holding area in memory where information can be stored. |
| Bug | An error in coding or logic that causes a program to malfunction. |
| Cache | A special memory subsystem in which frequently used data values are duplicated for quick access. |
| Cascade | The process of one action triggering another action. |

| | |
|---|---|
| Case-sensitive | Capable of distinguishing between uppercase and lowercase letters. |
| CD-ROM | Compact Disc - Read Only Memory; an optical disc which information may be read from but not written to. |
| Char data type | A data type that stores a fixed-length character string of length set by the Size property. |
| CGI | Common Gateway Interface - a convention for servers to communicate with local applications and allow users to provide information to scripts attached to web pages, usually through forms. |
| Class | The formal definition of an object. The class acts as the template from which an instance of an object is created at run time. |
| Class module | A module containing the definition of a class (its property and method definitions). |
| Click | To press and release a mouse button once without moving the mouse. |
| Client computer | A computer that accesses shared network resources provided by another server computer. |
| Code component | An .exe or .dll file that provides objects created from one of the classes the component provides. |
| Code module | A module containing public code that can be shared among all modules in a project. (Called a standard module in Visual Basic 6.0). |
| Code pane | A pane contained in a code window that is used for entering and editing code. A |

code window can contain one or more code panes.

COM                  Component Object Model. An industry-standard architecture for object-oriented development. It defines interfaces on which ActiveX components are built.

Command line         The path, file name, and argument information provided by the user to run a program.

Comment              Text added to code that explains how the code works. In Visual Basic, a comment line can start with either an apostrophe (') or with the Rem keyword followed by a space.

Compaction           A process that gathers or packs memory or storage into as small a space as possible.

Comparison operator  A character, or symbol, indicating a relationship between two or more values or expressions.

Compile error        An error that occurs during compile time as the result of incorrectly constructed code.

Compile time         The period during which source code is translated to executable code.

Configuration        A general purpose term referring to the way you have your computer set up.

Constant             A named item that retains a constant value throughout the execution of a program.

Context menu         A floating menu that is displayed over a form by right-clicking the mouse. Also called a pop-up menu.

| | |
|---|---|
| Control | An object you can place on a form that has its own set of recognised properties, methods, and events. |
| Control array | A group of controls that share a common name, type, and event procedures. |
| Currency data type | A data type that is used for calculations involving money or for fixed-point calculations of high accuracy. |
| Custom control | Now called an ActiveX control. |
| Data access page | A Web page, created by Access, that has a connection to a database; you can view, add, edit, and manipulate the data in this page. |
| Data source | The data the user wants to access and its associated operating system, DBMS, and network platform (if any). |
| Data type | The characteristics of a variable that determine what kind of data the variable can hold. |
| Database | A set of data related to a particular topic or purpose. A database contains tables and can also contain queries and table relationships, as well as validation criteria. |
| DBMS | (DataBase Management System). The software used to organise, analyse, and modify information stored in a database such as Microsoft Access. |
| Date data type | A data type used to store dates and times as a real number. |
| DDE | (Dynamic Data Exchange). A form of communications that uses shared memory to exchange data between applications. |

DDL

(Data Definition Language). The language used to describe, change, or define the attributes of a database, especially the layout of tables, columns, and their storage strategy.

Decimal data type

A data type that contains decimal numbers scaled by a power of 10.

Declaration

Non executable code that names a constant, variable, or procedure, and specifies its characteristics, such as its data type.

Default

The command, device or option automatically chosen.

Desktop

The Windows screen working background, on which you place icons, folders, etc.

Design time

The time during which you build or develop an application.

Dialogue box

A special window displayed by the system, or application, to obtain a response from or provide information to the user.

DLL

(Dynamic-Link Library). A set of routines that can be called from procedures and are loaded and linked into your application at run time.

Docked window

A window that is attached to the frame of the main window.

Document

Any self-contained work created with an application and given a unique file name.

Domain

A group of devices, servers and computers on a network.

| | |
|---|---|
| Double-click | To quickly press and release a mouse button twice. |
| Double data type | A data type that holds double-precision floating-point numbers. |
| Drag-and-drop | A combination of features that allow the user to drag an object and drop it onto a form or other object using the mouse. |
| Dynamic array | An array whose size can change at run time. |
| Dynaset | A type of Recordset object that returns a dynamic set of pointers to live database data. |
| EISA | Extended Industry Standard Architecture, for construction of PCs with the Intel 32-bit micro-processor. |
| Embedded object | An object whose data is stored along with that of its container but that runs in the process space of its server. |
| Error number | A whole number in the range 0 – 65,535, that corresponds to the Number property setting of the Err object. |
| Error trapping | The process of intercepting an error using error-handling features in Visual Basic. |
| Event | An action recognised by an object, such as clicking the mouse or pressing a key, and for which you can write code to respond. |
| Event procedure | A procedure automatically invoked in response to an event initiated by the user, program code, or the system. |

| | |
|---|---|
| Executable file | A Windows-based application that can run outside the development environment. An executable file has an .exe file name extension. |
| Expression | Any combination of operators, constants, literal values, functions, and names of fields, controls, and properties that evaluates to a single value. |
| FAT | The File Allocation Table. An area on disc where information is kept on which part of the disc a file is located. |
| Field | A category of information stored in a table in a database. |
| File extension | The suffix following the period in a filename. Windows uses this to identify the source application program. For example .mdb indicates an Access file. |
| Filename | The name given to a file. In Windows 95 and above this can be up to 256 characters long. |
| Filter | A set of criteria applied to rows in order to create a subset of the rows. |
| Firewall | Security measures designed to protect a networked system from unauthorised access. |
| Flag | A variable used to keep track of a condition in an application. You can set a flag using a constant or combination of constants. |
| Focus | The ability to receive mouse clicks or keyboard input at any one time. |
| Form | A window or dialogue box and a container for controls. |

| | |
|---|---|
| FTP | (File Transfer Protocol). A protocol for the transfer of files from one location to another over the Internet. |
| Function key | Any of the keys labelled F1 to F12. They often provide shortcuts for frequently carried out commands and actions. |
| Function procedure | A procedure that performs a specific task within a Visual Basic program and returns a value. |
| GIF | Graphics Interchange Format file. A graphics compressed bitmap format file developed for transmitting images over the Internet. |
| Graphics method | A method that operates on an object such as a Form, PictureBox, or Printer, and performs run-time drawing operations. |
| HTML | Hypertext Markup Language. The main language in which Web documents are written. |
| HTTP | Hypertext Transfer Protocol. The Internet protocol that delivers information over the Web. |
| Hyperlink | A location on a page from which a user can go to another page or location. Includes visible text or a graphic and the URL of the destination. |
| Hypermedia | Hypertext extended to include linked multimedia. |
| Hypertext | A system that allows documents to be cross-linked so that the reader can explore related links, or documents, by clicking on a highlighted symbol. |

| Icon | A graphical representation of an object or concept, as a bitmap with a maximum size of 32 x 32 pixels. |
| --- | --- |
| Index | A number that identifies an element in an array, control array, or collection. |
| Integer data type | A data type that holds integer variables stored as 2-byte whole numbers in the range – 32,768 to 32,767. |
| Internet | A worldwide network of thousands of smaller computer networks and millions of personal, commercial, educational, and government, computers. |
| Intranet | A network within an organisation that uses Internet technologies. |
| Intrinsic constant | A constant provided by an application. Visual Basic constants are listed in the Visual Basic object library and can be viewed using the Object Browser. |
| Intrinsic control | A standard control located on the Visual Basic Toolbox. |
| IP | Internet Protocol. The network layer for the TCP/IP protocol suite. |
| IP address | A 32-bit network address that uniquely identifies a system or device on an intranet or the Internet. |
| ISDN | (Integrated Services Digital Network). A telecom standard using digital transmission technology to support voice, video and data communications applications over regular telephone lines. |
| ISP | Internet Service Provider - A company that offers access to the Internet. |
| Java | An object-oriented programming language created by Sun Microsystems |

for developing applications and applets that are capable of running on any computer, regardless of the operating system.

JPG — Joint Photographic Experts Group (JPEG) file. A graphics file format supported by most browsers that was developed for compressing and storing photographic images.

Keyword — A word, or symbol, recognised as part of the Visual Basic programming language.

Line-continuation — The combination of a space followed by an underscore ( _ ) used in the code editor to extend a single logical line of code to two or more physical lines.

Linked object — An object that is created in another application and linked to a Visual Basic application.

Locked — The condition of a data page, row, Recordset object, or Database object, that makes it read-only to all users except the one currently entering data.

Logic error — A programming error that can cause code to produce incorrect results or stop execution.

MDI — Multiple-Document Interface application, with an MDI form as the container for any MDI child forms in the application.

Megabyte — (MB); 1024 kilobytes of information or storage space.

Megahertz — (MHz); Speed of processor in millions of cycles per second.

Message — A packet of information passed from one application to another.

| | |
|---|---|
| Method | A procedure that acts on an object. |
| MIDI | (Musical Instrument Digital Interface) - enables devices to transmit and receive sound and music messages. |
| MIME | (Multipurpose Internet Mail Extensions). A messaging standard that allows Internet users to exchange e-mail messages enhanced with graphics, video and voice. |
| MIPS | (Million Instructions Per Second). Measures the speed of a system. |
| Modem | Short for Modulator-demodulator devices. An electronic device that lets computers communicate electronically. |
| Monitor | The display device connected to your PC, also called a screen. |
| Module | A set of declarations followed by procedures. |
| MPEG | (Motion Picture Experts Group). A video file format offering excellent quality in a relatively small file. |
| Multi-tasking | Performing more than one operation at the same time. |
| Network | Two or more computers connected together to share resources. |
| Network server | Central computer which stores files for several linked computers. |
| Node | Any single computer connected to a network. |
| Numeric expression | Any expression that can be evaluated as a number. Elements of the expression can include any combination of keywords, variables, constants, and operators that result in a number. |

| | |
|---|---|
| Object | A combination of code and data that can be treated as a unit, for example, a control, form, or application component. Each object is defined by a class. |
| Object Browser | A dialogue box in which you can examine the contents of an object library to get information about the objects provided in it. |
| Object library | A dynamic-link library (DLL) with one or more type library resources that typically has the extension .olb. You can use the Object Browser to view its contents. |
| Object module | A module that contains code specific to an object. |
| ODBC | (Open Database Connectivity). A standard protocol that permits applications to connect to a variety of external database servers or files. |
| OLE | (Object Linking and Embedding). A special case of ActiveX that enables applications to be created that contain components from various other applications. |
| Parse | To identify the parts of a statement or expression and then validate those parts against the appropriate language rules. |
| Path | The location of a file in the folder, or directory, tree. |
| Pixel | Short for 'picture element'; a dot that represents the smallest graphic unit of measurement on a screen. |
| Plug-and-play | Hardware which can be plugged into a PC and that can be used immediately without configuration. |

| | |
|---|---|
| Point | In typography, a point is 1/72 of an inch. The size of a font is usually expressed in points. |
| POP | (Post Office Protocol). A method of storing and returning e-mail. |
| Pop-up menu | See context menu. |
| Print zone | Print zones begin every 14 columns. The width of each column is an average of the width of all characters in the point size for the selected font. |
| Private | Variables that are visible only to the module in which they are declared. |
| Procedure | A named sequence of statements executed as a unit. For example, Function, Property, and Sub are types of procedures. |
| Procedure template | The beginning and ending statements that are automatically inserted in the Code window when you specify a Sub, Function, or Property procedure. |
| Project | A Visual Basic program, or set of modules. |
| Project Explorer | A window that displays a list of files associated with a Visual Basic project or project group. |
| Project file | A file with a .vbp extension that keeps track of the files, objects, options, and references associated with a project. |
| Properties window | A window used to display or change properties of a selected form or control at design time. |
| Property | A named attribute of an object. |
| Public | Variables declared using the Public statement are visible to all procedures |

|  | in all modules in all applications unless Option Private Module is in effect. |
|---|---|
| Query | An instruction to a database to either return a set of records or perform a specified action on a set of records. |
| Read-only | A type of access to data where information can be retrieved but not modified. |
| Record | A set of related data about a person, place, event, or some other item. Table data is stored in records (rows) in a database. |
| Recursion | When a procedure calls itself. Uncontrolled recursion usually results in an 'Out of stack space' error message. |
| Registry | In Windows 95 and higher, the Windows registry serves as a central configuration database for user, application, and computer-specific information. |
| Relational | A type of database that stores information in tables. |
| Resource file | A file in a Visual Basic project with an .res file name extension that can contain bitmaps, text strings, or other data. |
| Restricted keyword | A word that Visual Basic uses as part of its language. |
| Run time | The time when an application is running. |
| Run-time error | An error that occurs when code is running. A run-time error results when a statement attempts an invalid operation. |
| Scope | The attribute of a variable or procedure that determines which sections of which |

modules recognise it.    Scope can be public, module, or procedure.

Server

The system designed to share data with client applications; servers and clients are often connected over a network.

Shortcut key

A function key or key combination, such as F5 or <Ctrl+A>, that executes a command.

Single data type

A data type that stores single-precision floating-point variables as 32-bit (2-byte) floating-point numbers.

SDI

(Single Document Interface). An application that can support only one document at a time.

SLIP

(Serial Line Internet Protocol). A method of Internet connection that enables computers to use phone lines and a modem to connect to the Internet without having to connect to a host.

Socket

An endpoint for sending and receiving data between computers.

Stack

A fixed amount of memory used by Visual Basic to preserve local variables and arguments during procedure calls.

Standard control

An intrinsic control included in the Visual Basic Toolbox.

Startup object

The first form displayed in an application, which is usually the first form created in the development environment.

Statement

A syntactically complete unit that expresses one kind of action, declaration, or definition, usually in a single line of code.

| | |
|---|---|
| Static | A Visual Basic keyword you can use to preserve the value of a local variable. |
| String constant | Any constant consisting of a sequence of contiguous characters interpreted as the characters themselves rather than as a numeric value. |
| String data type | A data type consisting of a sequence of contiguous characters that can include letters, numbers, spaces, and punctuation. The dollar sign ($) type-declaration character represents a String in Visual Basic. |
| String expression | Any expression that evaluates to a sequence of contiguous characters. |
| String literal | Any expression consisting of a sequence of contiguous characters surrounded by quotation marks that is literally interpreted as the characters within the quotation marks. |
| SQL | (Structured Query Language). A language used in querying, updating, and managing relational databases. |
| Sub procedure | A procedure that performs a specific task within a program, but returns no explicit value. |
| Syntax | The prescribed order and punctuation for putting programming language elements into statements that are meaningful to Visual Basic. |
| Syntax error | An error that occurs when you enter a line of code that Visual Basic doesn't recognise. |
| System modal | Describes a window, or dialogue box, that requires the user to take some action. |

| | |
|---|---|
| Tab order | The order in which the focus moves from one field to the next as the Tab or \<Shift+Tab\> keys are pressed. |
| Table | The basic unit of data storage in a relational database. A table stores data in records (rows) and fields (columns). |
| TCP/IP | (Transmission Control Protocol/Internet Protocol). The Internet standard for transferring data among networked computers. |
| Text data type | A field data type. |
| Time data type | A data type that stores a time value. The value is dependent on the clock setting of the data source. |
| Time expression | Any expression that can be interpreted as a time. |
| Toggle | To turn an action on and off with the same switch. |
| Twip | A screen-independent unit used to ensure that placement and proportion of screen elements in your screen application are the same on all display systems. A twip is a unit of screen measurement equal to 1/20 of a printer's point. |
| Type-declaration | A character appended to a variable name indicating the variable's data type. |
| URL | (Uniform Resource Locator). An address to an object, document, or page or other destination on the Internet or an intranet. |
| User-defined type | Any data type defined using the Type statement. |

| | |
|---|---|
| VarBinary data type | A data type that stores variable-length binary data. The maximum length is 255 bytes. |
| Variable | A named storage location that can contain data that can be modified during program execution. Each variable has a name that uniquely identifies it within its scope. |
| Variant data type | A special data type that can contain numeric, string, or date data as well as the special values Empty and Null. |
| Variant expression | Any expression that can evaluate to numeric, string, or date data as well as the special values Empty and Null. |
| VBScript | (Visual Basic Script). Microsoft's Internet scripting technology, based on Visual Basic |
| Virus | A malicious program, downloaded from a web site or disc, designed to wipe out information on your computer. |
| WAIS | (Wide Area Information Server). A Net-wide system for looking up specific information in Internet databases. |
| Watch expression | A user-defined expression that enables you to observe the behaviour of a variable or expression in the Watch window of the Visual Basic Editor. |
| WAV | Waveform Audio (.wav) - a common audio file format for DOS/Windows computers. |
| Wildcard characters | The asterisk (*), question mark (?), hash sign (#), exclamation mark (!), hyphen (-), and brackets ([ ]) can all be wildcard characters. They can be used in queries and expressions to include all records, file names, or other items that |

| | |
|---|---|
| | begin with specific characters or match a certain pattern. |
| Windows API | The Windows Application Programming Interface consists of the functions, messages, data structures, data types, and statements you can use in creating applications that run under Microsoft Windows. |
| WinSock | Windows Sockets is a standard way for Windows-based programs to work with TCP/IP. |
| Wizard | A tool that helps create an executable file by asking questions and then creating a file based on the answers. |
| Working directory | A specified directory on a local computer used to store files when they are checked out of the version control program's database. |
| World Wide Web | A system for navigating the Internet by using hyperlinks. With a browser, such as Internet Explorer, the Web appears as a collection of documents, controls, pictures, sounds, and digital movies. |
| Yes/No data type | A column data type that contains a Boolean (True/False or yes/no) value. |

# Appendix A

## The Code for VatCalc.vbp

All the code and property details for the two forms of the example program **VatCalc.vbp** are included here. As you may have noticed, Visual Basic 6.0 .frm files are saved in text format. All you need to do to look inside them is to open them in Notepad, or another text editor. You could also create them in this way as well. In the code below, some extra formatting has been added to make it easier to follow.

**NOTE** - Where one line of code will not fit on the book page, the Visual Basic continuation character ' _' has been placed at the end of the book line.

```
Begin VB.Form frmVatCalc
    Appearance      =   0   'Flat
    BorderStyle     =   1   'Fixed Single
    Caption         =   "VAT Calculator"
    ClientHeight    =   3465
    ClientLeft      =   1860
    ClientTop       =   2085
    ClientWidth     =   4005
    BeginProperty Font
        Name            =   "MS Sans Serif"
        Size            =   8.25
        Charset         =   0
        Weight          =   700
        Underline       =   0   'False
        Italic          =   0   'False
        Strikethrough   =   0   'False
    EndProperty
    ForeColor       =   &H80000008&
    LinkTopic       =   "Form1"
    MaxButton       =   0   'False
    PaletteMode     =   1   'UseZOrder
```

```
ScaleHeight      =    3465
ScaleWidth       =    4005

Begin VB.TextBox Text3
   Appearance    =    0    'Flat
   BackColor     =    &H8000000F&
   BorderStyle   =    0    'None
   Height        =    285
   Left          =    2760
   TabIndex      =    7
   TabStop       =    0    'False
   Top           =    1080
   Width         =    1215
End

Begin VB.TextBox Text2
   Appearance    =    0    'Flat
   BackColor     =    &H8000000F&
   BorderStyle   =    0    'None
   Height        =    285
   Left          =    2760
   TabIndex      =    8
   TabStop       =    0    'False
   Top           =    720
   Width         =    1215
End

Begin VB.CommandButton Command1
   Appearance    =    0    'Flat
   Caption       =    "&Calculate"
   Default       =    -1   'True
   Height        =    375
   Left          =    1200
   TabIndex      =    2
   Top           =    1560
   Width         =    1215
End

Begin VB.CommandButton Command3
   Appearance    =    0    'Flat
   Caption       =    "C&lear"
   Height        =    375
   Left          =    1200
```

```
        TabIndex        =    3
        Top             =    2760
        Width           =    1215
End

Begin VB.CommandButton Command2
        Appearance      =    0   'Flat
        Caption         =    "&Exit"
        Height          =    375
        Left            =    1200
        TabIndex        -    4
        Top             =    2160
        Width           =    1215
End

Begin VB.TextBox Text1
        Appearance      =    0   'Flat
        BackColor       =    &H8000000F&
        ForeColor       =    &H00000000&
        Height          =    285
        Left            =    2160
        TabIndex        =    0
        Top             =    240
        Width           =    1335
End

Begin VB.Label Label1
        Appearance      =    0   'Flat
        Caption         =    "Enter amount"
        ForeColor       =    &H80000008&
        Height          =    255
        Left            =    840
        TabIndex        =    1
        Top             =    240
        Width           =    1215
End

Begin VB.Label Label3
        Appearance      =    0   'Flat
        ForeColor       =    &H80000008&
        Height          =    255
        Left            =    240
        TabIndex        =    6
```

```
                Top           =    1080
                Width         =    2415
        End

        Begin VB.Label Label2
            Appearance        =    0    'Flat
            ForeColor         =    &H80000008&
            Height            =    255
            Left              =    240
            TabIndex          =    5
            Top               =    720
            Width             =    2295
        End

        Begin VB.Menu mnuOptions
            Caption           =    "&Options"
            Begin VB.Menu mnuVATRate
                Caption           =    "&VAT Rate"
            End
            Begin VB.Menu mnuAbout
                Caption           =    "&About"
            End
            Begin VB.Menu mnuExit
                Caption           =    "E&xit"
            End
        End
    End

Attribute VB_Name = "frmVatCalc"
Attribute VB_GlobalNameSpace = False
Attribute VB_Creatable = False
Attribute VB_PredeclaredId = True
Attribute VB_Exposed = False
Option Explicit
Dim Cost As Currency
Dim CostPlus As Currency
Dim Costless As Currency
Dim VATRate As Double
Dim NVATRate As Double

Private Sub Command1_Click()
    If NVATRate > 0 Then
        VATRate = NVATRate
```

```
    Else: VATRate = 17.5
    End If
    Cost = Val(Text1.Text)
    CostPlus = Cost * (1 + VATRate / 100)
    Costless = Cost / (1 + VATRate / 100)

    MsgPlus = "Amount plus " & VATRate & "% VAT = "
    MsgLess = "Amount less " & VATRate & "% VAT = "
    Label2.Caption = MsgPlus
    Text2.Text = CostPlus
    Label3.Caption = MsgLess
    Text3.Text = Costless

    Text1.Text = Format$(Cost, "currency")
    Text2.Text = Format$(CostPlus, "currency")
    Text3.Text = Format$(Costless, "currency")

End Sub

Private Sub Command2_Click()
    End    ' Leave the VAT calculater
End Sub

Private Sub Command3_Click() 'Clear text areas
    Text1.Text = ""
    Text2.Text = ""
    Text3.Text = ""
    Label2.Caption = ""
    Label3.Caption = ""
    Text1.SetFocus
End Sub

Private Sub mnuAbout_Click()

    frmAbout.Show 1

End Sub

Private Sub mnuExit_Click()
    End    ' Leave the VAT calculater
End Sub

Private Sub mnuVATRate_Click()
NVATRate = Val(InputBox$("Enter new VAT rate"))
VATRate = NVATRate
End Sub
```

```
Begin VB.Form frmAbout
   BorderStyle      =   3   'Fixed Dialog
   Caption          =   "About VatCalc"
   ClientHeight     =   3555
   ClientLeft       =   2340
   ClientTop        =   1935
   ClientWidth      =   5730
   ClipControls     =   0   'False
   LinkTopic        =   "Form2"
   MaxButton        =   0   'False
   MinButton        =   0   'False
   ScaleHeight      =   2453.724
   ScaleMode        =   0   'User
   ScaleWidth       =   5380.766
   ShowInTaskbar    =   0   'False

   Begin VB.PictureBox picIcon
      AutoSize         =   -1  'True
      ClipControls     =   0   'False
      Height           =   540
      Left             =   240
      Picture          =   "ABOUT.frx":0000
      ScaleHeight      =   337.12
      ScaleMode        =   0   'User
      ScaleWidth       =   337.12
      TabIndex         =   1
      Top              =   240
      Width            =   540
   End

   Begin VB.CommandButton cmdOK
      Cancel           =   -1  'True
      Caption          =   "OK"
      Default          =   -1  'True
      Height           =   345
      Left             =   4245
      TabIndex         =   0
      Top              =   2625
      Width            =   1260
   End
```

```
Begin VB.CommandButton cmdSysInfo
    Caption         =   "&System Info..."
    Height          =   345
    Left            =   4260
    TabIndex        =   2
    Top             =   3075
    Width           =   1245
End

Begin VB.Line Line1
    BorderColor     =   &H00808080&
    BorderStyle     =   6   'Inside Solid
    Index           =   1
    X1              =   84.515
    X2              =   5309.398
    Y1              =   1687.583
    Y2              =   1687.583
End

Begin VB.Label lblDescription
    Caption         =   $"ABOUT.frx":030A
    ForeColor       =   &H00000000&
    Height          =   1170
    Left            =   1050
    TabIndex        =   3
    Top             =   1125
    Width           =   3885
End

Begin VB.Label lblTitle
    ForeColor       =   &H00000000&
    Height          =   480
    Left            =   1050
    TabIndex        =   5
    Top             =   240
    Width           =   3885
End

Begin VB.Line Line1
    BorderColor     =   &H00FFFFFF&
    BorderWidth     =   2
    Index           =   0
    X1              =   98.6
```

```
        X2              =    5309.398
        Y1              =    1697.936
        Y2              =    1697.936
     End

     Begin VB.Label lblVersion
        Height          =    225
        Left            =    1050
        TabIndex        =    6
        Top             =    780
        Width           =    3885
     End

     Begin VB.Label lblDisclaimer
        Caption         =    "No Copyright restrictions _
        apply"
        ForeColor       =    &H00000000&
        Height          =    825
        Left            =    255
        TabIndex        =    4
        Top             =    2625
        Width           =    3870
     End
  End
End
Attribute VB_Name = "frmAbout"
Attribute VB_GlobalNameSpace = False
Attribute VB_Creatable = False
Attribute VB_PredeclaredId = True
Attribute VB_Exposed = False
Option Explicit

' Reg Key Security Options...
Const READ_CONTROL = &H20000
Const KEY_QUERY_VALUE = &H1
Const KEY_SET_VALUE = &H2
Const KEY_CREATE_SUB_KEY = &H4
Const KEY_ENUMERATE_SUB_KEYS = &H8
Const KEY_NOTIFY = &H10
Const KEY_CREATE_LINK = &H20
Const KEY_ALL_ACCESS = KEY_QUERY_VALUE + _
KEY_SET_VALUE + KEY_CREATE_SUB_KEY + -
KEY_ENUMERATE_SUB_KEYS + _
KEY_NOTIFY + KEY_CREATE_LINK + READ_CONTROL
```

```
' Reg Key ROOT Types...
Const HKEY_LOCAL_MACHINE = &H80000002
Const ERROR_SUCCESS = 0
Const REG_SZ = 1          'Unicode nul terminated string
Const REG_DWORD = 4       '32-bit number

Const gREGKEYSYSINFOLOC = "SOFTWARE\Microsoft\Shared _
Tools Location"
Const gREGVALSYSINFOLOC = "MSINFO"
Const gREGKEYSYSINFO = "SOFTWARE\Microsoft\Shared _
Tools\MSINFO"
Const gREGVALSYSINFO = "PATH"

Private Declare Function RegOpenKeyEx Lib "advapi32" _
Alias "RegOpenKeyExA" (ByVal hKey As Long, _
ByVal lpSubKey As String, ByVal ulOptions As Long, _
ByVal samDesired As Long, _
ByRef phkResult As Long) As Long
Private Declare Function RegQueryValueEx Lib _
"advapi32" Alias "RegQueryValueExA" (ByVal hKey As _
Long, ByVal lpValueName As String, ByVal lpReserved _
As Long, ByRef lpType As Long, _
ByVal lpData As String, ByRef lpcbData As Long) As Long
Private Declare Function RegCloseKey Lib "advapi32" _
(ByVal hKey As Long) As Long

Private Sub cmdSysInfo_Click()
  Call StartSysInfo
End Sub

Private Sub cmdOK_Click()
  Unload Me
End Sub

Private Sub Form_Load()
    Me.Caption = "About " & App.Title
    lblVersion.Caption = "Version " & App.Major & "." _
    & App.Minor & "." & App.Revision & "    Nov. 2000"
    lblTitle.Caption = App.Title
End Sub


Public Sub StartSysInfo()
    On Error GoTo SysInfoErr
```

```
    Dim rc As Long
    Dim SysInfoPath As String

    ' Try To Get System Info Program Path\Name From
    ' Registry...
    If GetKeyValue(HKEY_LOCAL_MACHINE, _
    gREGKEYSYSINFO, gREGVALSYSINFO, SysInfoPath) Then
    ' Try To Get System Info Program Path Only From
    ' Registry...
    ElseIf GetKeyValue(HKEY_LOCAL_MACHINE, _
    gREGKEYSYSINFOLOC, gREGVALSYSINFOLOC, _
    SysInfoPath) Then
    ' Validate Existance Of Known 32 Bit File Version
        If (Dir(SysInfoPath & "\MSINFO32.EXE") <> "") _
        Then
            SysInfoPath = SysInfoPath & "\MSINFO32.EXE"

        ' Error - File Can Not Be Found...
        Else
            GoTo SysInfoErr
        End If
    ' Error - Registry Entry Can Not Be Found...
    Else
        GoTo SysInfoErr
    End If

    Call Shell(SysInfoPath, vbNormalFocus)

    Exit Sub

SysInfoErr:
    MsgBox "System Information Is Unavailable At This _
    Time", vbOKOnly
End Sub

Public Function GetKeyValue(KeyRoot As Long, KeyName _
As String, SubKeyRef As String, ByRef KeyVal _
As String) As Boolean
    Dim i As Long          ' Loop Counter
    Dim rc As Long         ' Return Code
    Dim hKey As Long       ' Handle To An Open Registry Key
    Dim hDepth As Long
    Dim KeyValType As Long ' Data Type Of A Registry Key
    Dim tmpVal As String
```

```
    ' Tempory Storage For A Registry Key Value
    Dim KeyValSize As Long
    ' Size Of Registry Key Variable


'---------------------------------------------------------
    ' Open RegKey Under KeyRoot {HKEY_LOCAL_MACHINE...}
'---------------------------------------------------------
    rc = RegOpenKeyEx(KeyRoot, KeyName, 0, _
    KEY_ALL_ACCESS, hKey) ' Open Registry Key

    If (rc <> ERROR_SUCCESS) Then GoTo GetKeyError
    ' Handle Error...

    tmpVal = String$(1024, 0)
    ' Allocate Variable Space
    KeyValSize = 1024
    ' Mark Variable Size


'---------------------------------------------------------
    ' Retrieve Registry Key Value...
'---------------------------------------------------------
    rc = RegQueryValueEx(hKey, SubKeyRef, 0, _
    KeyValType, tmpVal, KeyValSize)
    ' Get/Create Key Value

    If (rc <> ERROR_SUCCESS) Then GoTo GetKeyError
    ' Handle Errors

    If (Asc(Mid(tmpVal, KeyValSize, 1)) = 0) Then
    ' Win95 Adds Null Terminated String...
        tmpVal = Left(tmpVal, KeyValSize - 1)
    ' Null Found, Extract From String
    Else
    ' WinNT Does NOT Null Terminate String...
        tmpVal = Left(tmpVal, KeyValSize)
    ' Null Not Found, Extract String Only
    End If
```

```
'------------------------------------------------------
' Determine Key Value Type For Conversion...
'------------------------------------------------------
    Select Case KeyValType
    ' Search Data Types...
    Case REG_SZ
    ' String Registry Key Data Type
        KeyVal = tmpVal
    ' Copy String Value
    Case REG_DWORD
    ' Double Word Registry Key Data Type
        For i = Len(tmpVal) To 1 Step -1
    ' Convert Each Bit
            KeyVal = KeyVal + Hex(Asc(Mid(tmpVal, _
            i, 1)))    ' Build Value Char. By Char.
        Next
        KeyVal = Format$("&h" + KeyVal)
    ' Convert Double Word To String
    End Select

    GetKeyValue = True
    ' Return Success
    rc = RegCloseKey(hKey)
    ' Close Registry Key
    Exit Function

GetKeyError:    ' Cleanup After An Error Has Occured...
    KeyVal = ""
    ' Set Return Val To Empty String
    GetKeyValue = False
    ' Return Failure
    rc = RegCloseKey(hKey)
    ' Close Registry Key
End Function
```

# Appendix B

# Naming Conventions

This appendix presents a set of suggested coding conventions for Visual Basic programs, representing programming guidelines that focus not on the logic of the program but on its physical structure and appearance. They make the code easier to read, understand, and to maintain.

The main reason for using a consistent set of coding conventions is to standardise the structure and coding style of an application so that both you and other users can easily read and understand the code.

Good coding conventions result in precise, readable, and unambiguous source code that is consistent with other language conventions and is as intuitive as possible.

The names you give to forms and controls:

- Should begin with a letter.

- Should contain only letters, numbers, and the underscore character '_'. Punctuation characters and spaces are not allowed.

- Should be no longer than 40 characters.

## Object Naming Conventions

Objects should be named with a consistent prefix that makes it easy to identify the object's type. Recommended conventions, (as included in Microsoft's MSDN Library), for the main objects supported by Visual Basic are listed below. In this book we have only used a small proportion of these object types.

# Prefixes for Controls

| Control Type | Prefix | Example |
|---|---|---|
| 3D Panel | pnl | pnlGroup |
| ADO Data | ado | adoBiblio |
| Animated button | ani | aniMailBox |
| Check box | chk | chkReadOnly |
| Combo box | cbo | cboEnglish |
| Command button | cmd | cmdExit |
| Common dialogue | dlg | dlgFileOpen |
| Communications | com | comFax |
| Control (unknown type) | ctr | ctrCurrent |
| Data | dat | datBiblio |
| Data-bound combo box | dbcbo | dbcboLanguage |
| Data-bound grid | dbgrd | dbgrdQueryResult |
| Data-bound list box | dblst | dblstJobType |
| Data combo | dbc | dbcAuthor |
| Data grid | dgd | dgdTitles |
| Data list | dbl | dblPublisher |
| Data repeater | drp | drpLocation |
| Date picker | dtp | dtpPublished |
| Directory list box | dir | dirSource |
| Drive list box | drv | drvTarget |
| File list box | fil | filSource |
| Flat scroll bar | fsb | fsbMove |
| Form | frm | frmEntry |
| Frame | fra | fraLanguage |
| Gauge | gau | gauStatus |
| Graph | gra | graRevenue |
| Grid | grd | grdPrices |
| Hierarchical flexgrid | flex | flexOrders |
| Horizontal scroll bar | hsb | hsbVolume |
| Image | img | imgIcon |
| Image combo | imgcbo | imgcboProduct |
| ImageList | ils | ilsAllIcons |
| Label | lbl | lblHelpMessage |
| Lightweight check box | lwchk | lwchkArchive |
| Lightweight combo box | lwcbo | lwcboGerman |
| Lightweight cmd button | lwcmd | lwcmdRemove |

| | | |
|---|---|---|
| Lightweight frame | lwfra | lwfraSaveOptions |
| Lightweight hor. scroll bar | lwhsb | lwhsbVolume |
| Lightweight list box | lwlst | lwlstCostCenters |
| Lightweight option button | lwopt | lwoptIncomeLevel |
| Lightweight text box | lwtxt | lwoptStreet |
| Lightweight vert. scroll bar | lwvsb | lwvsbYear |
| Line | lin | linVertical |
| List box | lst | lstPolicyCodes |
| ListView | lvw | lvwHeadings |
| MAPI message | mpm | mpmSentMessage |
| MAPI session | mps | mpsSession |
| MCI | mci | mciVideo |
| Menu | mnu | mnuFileOpen |
| Month view | mvw | mvwPeriod |
| MS Chart | ch | chSalesbyRegion |
| MS Flex grid | msg | msgClients |
| MS Tab | mst | mstFirst |
| OLE container | ole | oleWorksheet |
| Option button | opt | optGender |
| Picture box | pic | picVGA |
| Picture clip | clp | clpToolbar |
| ProgressBar | prg | prgLoadFile |
| Remote Data | rd | rdTitles |
| RichTextBox | rtf | rtfReport |
| Shape | shp | shpCircle |
| Slider | sld | sldScale |
| Spin | spn | spnPages |
| StatusBar | sta | staDateTime |
| SysInfo | sys | sysMonitor |
| TabStrip | tab | tabOptions |
| Text box | txt | txtLastName |
| Timer | tmr | tmrAlarm |
| Toolbar | tlb | tlbActions |
| TreeView | tre | treOrganization |
| UpDown | upd | updDirection |
| Vertical scroll bar | vsb | vsbRate |

# Prefixes for Data Access Objects

| Database Object | Prefix | Example |
|---|---|---|
| Container | con | conReports |
| Database | db | dbAccounts |
| DBEngine | dbe | dbeJet |
| Document | doc | docSalesReport |
| Field | fld | fldAddress |
| Group | grp | grpFinance |
| Index | ix | idxAge |
| Parameter | prm | prmJobCode |
| QueryDef | qry | qrySalesByRegion |
| Recordset | rec | recForecast |
| Relation | rel | relEmployeeDept |
| TableDef | tbd | tbdCustomers |
| User | usr | usrNew |
| Workspace | wsp | wspMine |

# Prefixes for Menus

Applications frequently use many menu controls, making it useful to have a unique set of naming conventions for these controls. Menu control prefixes should be extended beyond the initial 'mnu' label by adding an additional prefix for each level of nesting, with the final menu caption at the end of the name string. The following table lists some examples.

| Menu Caption Sequence | Menu Handler Name |
|---|---|
| File Open | mnuFileOpen |
| File Send Email | mnuFileSendEmail |
| File Send Fax | mnuFileSendFax |
| Format Character | mnuFormatCharacter |
| Help Contents | mnuHelpContents |

When this naming convention is used, all members of a particular menu group are listed next to each other in Visual Basic's Properties window, and the menu control names clearly document the menu items to which they are attached.

# Naming Constants and Variables

As well as objects, constants and variables also require well-formed naming conventions. This section lists recommended conventions for constants and variables supported by Visual Basic.

Variables should always be defined with the smallest scope possible. Global (Public) variables can create enormously complex situations and make the logic of an application extremely difficult to understand. Global variables also make the re-use and maintenance of code much more difficult.

Variables in Visual Basic can have the following scope:

| Scope | Declaration | Visible in |
|---|---|---|
| Procedure-level | 'Private' in procedure, sub, or function | The procedure in which it is declared |
| Module-level | 'Private' in the declarations section of a form or code module (.frm, .bas) | Every procedure in the form or code module |
| Global | 'Public' in the declarations section of a code module (.bas) | Everywhere in the application |

In a Visual Basic application, global variables should be used only when there is no other convenient way to share data between forms. When global variables must be used, it is good practice to declare them all in a single module, grouped by function. The module should be given a meaningful name that indicates its purpose, such as Public.bas.

It is good coding practice to write modular code whenever possible. For example, if your application displays a dialogue box, put all the controls and code required to perform the dialogue's task in a single form. This helps to keep the application's code organised into useful components and minimises its run-time overhead.

As project size grows, so does the value of recognising variable scope quickly. A one-letter scope prefix preceding the type prefix provides this, without greatly increasing the size of variable names.

| Scope | Prefix | Example |
|---|---|---|
| Global | g | gstrUserName |
| Module-level | m | mblnCalcInProgress |
| Local to procedure | None | dblVelocity |

A variable has global scope if it is declared Public in a standard module or a form module; and module-level scope if declared Private in a standard module or form module.

The body of constant names should be mixed case with capitals initiating each word. Although standard Visual Basic constants do not include data type and scope information, especially for large programs, the prefix can be extended to indicate the scope of the variable, as follows.

| Data type | Prefix | Example |
|---|---|---|
| Boolean | bln | blnFound |
| Byte | byt | bytRasterData |
| Collection object | col | colWidgets |
| Currency | cur | curRevenue |
| Date (Time) | dtm | dtmStart |
| Double | dbl | dblTolerance |
| Error | err | errOrderNum |
| Integer | int | intQuantity |
| Long | lng | lngDistance |
| Object | obj | objCurrent |
| Single | sng | sngAverage |
| String | str | strFName |
| User-defined type | udt | udtEmployee |
| Variant | vnt | vntCheckSum |

# Appendix C

## User-Defined Formatting

With the system time at just after 5.08pm on 7th November 2000, the following Visual Basic and user-defined formats produced the output shown from our UK based PC:

| Format | Displays |
|--------|----------|
| Format(Now, "General Date") | 07/11/2000 05:08:20 |
| Format(Date, "General Date") | 07/11/2000 |
| Format(Date, "Long Date") | 07 November 2000 |
| Format(Date, "Medium Date") | 07-Nov-00 |
| Format(Date, "Short Date") | 07/11/2000 |
| Format(Time, "Long Time") | 05:08:20 |
| Format(Time, "Medium Time") | 05:08 PM |
| Format(Time, "Short Time") | 17:08 |
| Format(Now, "dddddd") | 07 November 2000 |
| Format(Now, "ttttt") | 05:08:20 |
| Format(Now, "d/m/yyyy") | 7/11/2000 |
| Format(Now, "d-mmmm-yy") | 7-November-00 |
| Format(Now, "d-mmmm") | 7 November |
| Format(Now, "mmmm-yy") | November 00 |
| Format(Now, "hh:mm AM/PM") | 05:08 PM |
| Format(Now, "h:mm:ss a/p") | 5:08:20 p |
| Format(Now, "h:mm") | 17:08 |
| Format(Now, "h:mm:ss") | 17:08:20 |
| Format(Now, "d/m /yy h:mm") | 7/11/00 17:08 |
| Format(Date, "dddd, d mmm yyyy") | Tuesday, 7 Nov 2000 |
| Format(Time, "h:m:s") | 17:8:20 |
| Format(Time, "hh:mm:ss AMPM") | 05:08:20 PM |
| Format(14) | 14 (but as the string "14") |
| Format(1233.4, "##,##0.00") | 1,233.40 |
| Format(368.9, "###0.00") | 368.90 |
| Format(0.5, "0.00%") | 50.00% |
| Format("HI THERE", "<") | hi there |
| Format("Thank you Fred", ">") | THANK YOU FRED |

Some date and time output formats depend on the country and personal settings of your system.

The following tables identify the characters you can use to create user-defined formats in your Visual Basic programs. They are all used with the Format function, as in our previous examples.

# User-Defined Numeric Formats

### *Character  Description*

| | |
|---|---|
| 0 | Digit placeholder. Display a digit or a zero |
| # | Digit placeholder. Display a digit or nothing. |
| . | Decimal placeholder |
| % | Percentage placeholder. The expression is multiplied by 100. The percent character (%) is inserted in the position where it appears in the format string. |
| , | Thousand separator |
| : | Time separator. Separates hours, minutes, and seconds when time values are formatted. This is determined by your system settings. |
| / | Date separator. Separates the day, month, and year when date values are formatted. This is determined by your system settings. |
| E- E+ e- e+ | Scientific format. If the format expression contains at least one digit placeholder (0 or #) to the right of E-, E+, e-, or e+, the number is displayed in scientific format and E or e is inserted between the number and its exponent. |
| - + $ ( ) | Display a literal character. To display a character other than one of those listed, precede it with a backslash (\) or enclose it in double quotation marks (" "). |
| \ | Display the next character in the format string To display a backslash, use two backslashes (\\). |

"ABC"        Display the string inside the double quotation
             marks (" "). To include a string in format from
             within code, you must use Chr(34) to enclose
             the text (34 is the character code for a
             quotation mark (")).

# User-Defined Date/Time Formats

*Character*    *Description*

:            Time separator.

/            Date separator.

c            Display the date as ddddd and display the time
             as ttttt, in that order. Display only date
             information if there is no fractional part to the
             date serial number; display only time
             information if there is no integer portion.

d            Display the day as a number without a leading
             zero (1 – 31).

dd           Display the day as a number with a leading
             zero (01 – 31).

ddd          Display the day as an abbreviation (Sun – Sat).

dddd         Display the day as a full name,
             (Sunday – Saturday).

ddddd        Display the date as a complete date (including
             day, month, and year), formatted according to
             your system's short date format setting. The
             default short date format is m/d/yy.

dddddd       Display a date serial number as a complete
             date (including day, month, and year) formatted
             according to the long date setting recognized
             by your system. The default long date format is
             mmmm dd, yyyy.

| | |
|---|---|
| w | Display the day of the week as a number (1 for Sunday through 7 for Saturday). |
| ww | Display the week of the year as a number (1 – 54). |
| m | Display the month as a number without a leading zero (1 – 12). If m immediately follows h or hh, the minute rather than the month is displayed. |
| mm | Display the month as a number with a leading zero (01 – 12). If m immediately follows h or hh, the minute rather than the month is displayed. |
| mmm | Display the month as an abbreviation (Jan – Dec). |
| mmmm | Display the month as a full month name (January – December). |
| q | Display the quarter of the year as a number (1 – 4). |
| y | Display the day of the year as a number (1 – 366). |
| yy | Display the year as a 2-digit number (00 – 99). |
| yyyy | Display the year as a 4-digit number (100 – 9999). |
| h | Display the hour as a number without leading zeros (0 – 23). |
| Hh | Display the hour as a number with leading zeros (00 – 23). |
| N | Display the minute as a number without leading zeros (0 – 59). |
| Nn | Display the minute as a number with leading zeros (00 – 59). |
| S | Display the second as a number without leading zeros (0 – 59). |

| | |
|---|---|
| Ss | Display the second as a number with leading zeros (00 – 59). |
| ttttt | Display a time as a complete time (including hour, minute, and second), formatted using the time separator defined by the time format recognized by your system. The default time format is h:mm:ss. |
| AM/PM | Use the 12-hour clock and display an uppercase AM with any hour before noon; and an upperoase PM with any hour between noon and 11:59 P.M. |
| am/pm | Use the 12-hour clock and display a lowercase AM with any hour before noon; and a lowercase PM with any hour between noon and 11:59 P.M. |
| A/P | Use the 12-hour clock and display an uppercase A with any hour before noon; display an uppercase P with any hour between noon and 11:59 P.M. |
| a/p | Use the 12-hour clock and display a lowercase A with any hour before noon; display a lowercase P with any hour between noon and 11:59 P.M. |
| AMPM | Use the 12-hour clock and display the AM string literal as defined by your system with any hour before noon; and display the PM string literal as defined by your system with any hour between noon and 11:59 P.M. |

# User-Defined String Formats

### *Character Description*

@          Character placeholder. Display a character or a space. If the string has a character in the position where the @ appears in the format string, it is displayed.

&          Character placeholder. Display a character or nothing.

<          Force lowercase. Display all characters in lowercase format.

>          Force uppercase. Display all characters in uppercase format.

!          Force left to right fill of placeholders. The default is to fill placeholders from right to left.

# Appendix D

# Language Reference

## Event Procedures

The following is an alphabetic list of the event triggered procedures of Visual Basic you are most likely to use. An event is an action which is recognised by a form or control. The event name is substituted in the procedure declaration as follows:

**Sub** ControlName_**EventName** (arguments)

| *Event* | *Description* |
|---|---|
| Activate | Occurs when an object becomes the active window. |
| ButtonClick | Occurs when the user clicks on a Button object in a Toolbar control. |
| Change | Indicates that the contents of a control have changed. |
| Click | Occurs when the user clicks (presses and then releases) a mouse button over an object. |
| DateClick | Occurs when a date on the control is clicked. |
| DblClick | Occurs when the user quickly double clicks a mouse button over an object. |
| Deactivate | Occurs when an object is no longer the active window. |
| DonePainting | Occurs immediately after the chart repaints or redraws. |
| DownClick | Occurs when the down or left arrow button are clicked. |

| | |
|---|---|
| DragDrop | Occurs when a drag-and-drop operation is completed by dragging a control over a form or other control. |
| DragOver | Occurs when a drag-and-drop operation is in progress. Can be used to monitor when the mouse pointer enters, leaves, or is directly over a valid target. |
| DropDown | Occurs when the list portion of a combo box is about to drop down; this event does not occur if a combo box's Style property is set to 1 (Simple Combo). |
| EnterCell | Occurs when the currently active cell changes to a different cell. |
| EnterFocus | Occurs when focus enters the object. |
| Error | Occurs as the result of a data access error that occurs when no Visual Basic code is being executed. |
| ExitFocus | Occurs when focus leaves the object. |
| GotFocus | Occurs when an object receives the focus, either by tabbing to or clicking on the object, or with the SetFocus method in code. |
| KeyDown | Occurs when the user presses a key while an object has the focus. Used with the KeyPress event. |
| KeyPress | Occurs when the user presses and releases an ANSI code key. |
| KeyUp | Occurs when the user releases a key while an object has the focus. Used with the KeyPress event. |
| LinkClose | Occurs when a DDE conversation terminates. |
| LinkError | Occurs when there is an error during a DDE conversation. |

| | |
|---|---|
| LinkExecute | Occurs when a command string is sent by a destination application in a DDE conversation. |
| LinkNotify | Occurs when the source has changed the data defined by the DDE link, (destination LinkMode property set to 3 - Notify). |
| LinkOpen | Occurs when a DDE conversation is being initiated. |
| Load | Occurs when a form is loaded. |
| LostFocus | Occurs when an object loses the focus, either by tabbing to or clicking on the object, or in code with the SetFocus method. |
| MouseDown | Occurs when the user presses a mouse button. |
| MouseMove | Occurs when the user moves the mouse. |
| MouseUp | Occurs when the user releases a mouse button. |
| Paint | Occurs when part, or all, of a form or picturebox is exposed after it has been moved or enlarged, or after a window that was covering the object has been moved. |
| PathChange | Occurs when the path changes by setting the FileName or Path properties from code. |
| PatternChange | Occurs when the file filter (e.g. *.*) has changed by setting the FileName or Pattern properties from code. |
| QueryUnload | Occurs before a form or application closes. |
| Reposition | Occurs after a record becomes the current record. |
| Resize | Occurs when a form first appears or the size of an object changes. |
| RowColChange | Occurs when the currently active cell changes to a different cell. |
| Scroll | Occurs while a user drags the box on a scroll bar. |

| | |
|---|---|
| SelChange | Occurs when the selected range changes to a different cell or range of cells. |
| Timer | Occurs when a preset interval for a timer control has elapsed. |
| Unload | Occurs when a form is about to be removed from the screen. |
| UpClick | Occurs when the up or right arrow button is clicked. |
| Updated | Occurs when an object's data has been modified. |
| User | Occurs in response to the firing of a run-time defined event. |
| Validate | Occurs before the focus shifts to a (second) control that has its CausesValidation property set to True. |

# Main Visual Basic Keywords

The following are listings of Visual Basic's main function, statement and method key-words. Where a **function** is a standard procedure that performs a specific task and returns a value; a **statement** is a reserved word which forms part of a complete expression indicating one kind of action, declaration, or definition; and a **method** is a Visual Basic reserved word that acts on a particular object.

In the first section the keywords are grouped in an alphabetical listing of the main tasks you are likely to perform in Visual Basic. In the second, they are just listed alphabetically with a short description.

First find the available commands for the operation you are carrying out, then for more detailed information, look in the alphabetical details list at the end of this Appendix. Then we suggest you search the reference section of the Visual Basic Help facility. This includes working examples of them all.

## Listed by Programming Task

| *Action* | *Keywords* |
| --- | --- |
| **Arrays** | |
| Change default lower limit | **Option Base** |
| Declare and initialise | **Dim, Private** |
| | **Public, ReDim** |
| | **Static** |
| Find the limits | **Lbound, Ubound** |
| Reinitialise | **Erase, ReDim** |
| Verify and create | **IsArray, Array** |
| **Controlling Program Flow** | |
| Branch | **GoSub...Return** |
| | **GoTo** |
| | **On Error** |
| | **On...GoSub** |
| | **On...GoTo** |
| Exit or pause the program | **DoEvents, End** |
| | **Exit, Stop** |

| | |
|---|---|
| Loop | **Do...Loop** |
| | **For...Next** |
| | **For Each...Next** |
| | **While...Wend, With** |
| Make decisions | **Choose, Switch** |
| | **If...Then...Else** |
| | **Select Case** |
| Use procedures | **Call, Function** |
| | **Property Get** |
| | **Property Let** |
| | **Property Set, Sub** |

**Conversion**

| | |
|---|---|
| ANSI value to string | **Chr, Chr$** |
| String to lower or upper case | **Format, Lcase** |
| | **Ucase** |
| Date to serial number | **DateSerial** |
| | **DateValue** |
| Decimal numbers to other bases | **Hex, Hex$** |
| | **Oct, Oct$** |
| Number to string | **Format, Format$** |
| | **Str, Str$** |
| One data type to another | **CBool, CByte, CCur** |
| | **CDate, CDbl, CDec** |
| | **CInt, CLng, CSng** |
| | **Cstr, CVar, CVerr** |
| | **Fix, Int** |
| Serial number to date | **Day, Month** |
| | **Weekday, Year** |
| Serial number to time | **Hour, Minute** |
| | **Second** |
| String to ASCII value | **Asc** |
| String to number | **Val** |
| Time to serial number | **TimeSerial,** |
| | **TimeValue** |

**Cutting, Copying, and Pasting**

| | |
|---|---|
| Use the Clipboard object | **Clear, GetData** |
| | **GetFormat, GetText** |
| | **SetData, SetText** |

## Data Types

| | |
|---|---|
| Convert between data types | **CBool, CByte, Ccur** |
| | **CDate, CDbl, Cdec** |
| | **Cint, CLng, Csng** |
| | **CStr, Cvar, CVErr** |
| | **Fix, Int** |
| Set intrinsic data types | **Boolean, Byte** |
| | **Currency, Date** |
| | **Double Integer** |
| | **Long, Object** |
| | **Single, String** |
| | **Variant** |
| Verify data types | **IsArray, IsDate** |
| | **IsEmpty, IsError** |
| | **IsMissing, IsNull** |
| | **IsNumeric, IsObject** |

## Dates and Times

| | |
|---|---|
| Get current date or time | **Date, Date$, Now** |
| | **Time, Time$** |
| Perform date calculations | **DateAdd, DateDiff** |
| | **DatePart** |
| Return a date | **DateSerial** |
| | **DateValue** |
| Return a time | **TimeSerial** |
| | **TimeValue** |
| Set the date or time | **Date, Date$** |
| | **Time, Time$** |
| Time a process | **Timer** |

## Error Trapping

| | |
|---|---|
| Generate runtime errors | **Clear, Error, Raise** |
| Get error messages | **Error** |
| Get error-status data | **Err** |
| Return error variant | **CVErr** |
| Trap errors while running | **On Error, Resume** |
| Type verification | **IsError** |

### File Input/Output

| | |
|---|---|
| Access or create a file | **Open** |
| Close files | **Close, Reset** |
| Control output appearance | **Format, Print** |
| | **Print #, Spc** |
| | **Tab, Width #** |
| Copy one file to another | **FileCopy** |
| Get information about a file | **EOF, FileAttr** |
| | **FileDateTime** |
| | **FileLen, FreeFile** |
| | **GetAttr, Loc** |
| | **LOF, Seek** |
| Manage disc drives or directories | **ChDir, ChDrive** |
| | **CurDir, CurDir$** |
| | **MkDir, RmDir** |
| Manage files | **Dir, Kill** |
| | **Lock, Unlock, Name** |
| Read from a file | **Get, Input, Input #** |
| | **Line Input #** |
| Return file length | **FileLen** |
| Set or get file attributes | **FilAttr, GetAttr** |
| | **SetAttr** |
| Set read-write position in a file | **Seek** |
| Write to a file | **Print #, Put, Write #** |

### Financial

| | |
|---|---|
| Calculate depreciation | **DDB, SLN, SYD** |
| Calculate future value | **FV** |
| Calculate interest rate | **Rate** |
| Calculate internal rate of return | **IRR, MIRR** |
| Calculate number of periods | **NPer** |
| Calculate payments | **IPmt, Pmt, PPmt** |
| Calculate present value | **NPV, PV** |

### Graphics

| | |
|---|---|
| Change coordinate system | **Scale** |
| Clear run-time graphics | **Cls** |
| Draw shapes | **Circle, Line, PSet** |
| Draw text | **Print** |

Find size of text · · · · · · · · · · · · · · · · · · · · **TextHeight**
· · · · · · · · · · · · · · · · · · · · · · · · · · · · · · · **TextWidth**
Load or save a picture file · · · · · · · · · · · · · **LoadPicture**
· · · · · · · · · · · · · · · · · · · · · · · · · · · · · · · **SavePicture**
Work with colours · · · · · · · · · · · · · · · · · · · · **Point, QBColor**
· · · · · · · · · · · · · · · · · · · · · · · · · · · · · · · **RGB**

## Manipulating Objects

Arrange forms or controls
on the screen · · · · · · · · · · · · · · · · · · · · · · **Arrange, ZOrder**
Direct user input to a control · · · · · · · · · · · · **SetFocus**
Display dialogue boxes · · · · · · · · · · · · · · · · **InputBox, MsgBox**
Drag and drop · · · · · · · · · · · · · · · · · · · · · · **Drag**
Hide or show forms · · · · · · · · · · · · · · · · · · · **Hide, Show**
Load or unload objects · · · · · · · · · · · · · · · · **Load, Unload**
Move or re-size controls · · · · · · · · · · · · · · · **Move**
Print forms · · · · · · · · · · · · · · · · · · · · · · · · · **PrintForm**
Update the display · · · · · · · · · · · · · · · · · · · **Refresh**
Work with list and combo boxes · · · · · · · · · · **AddItem**
· · · · · · · · · · · · · · · · · · · · · · · · · · · · · · · **RemoveItem**

## Mathematical

General calculations · · · · · · · · · · · · · · · · · · **Exp, Log, Sqr**
Generate random numbers · · · · · · · · · · · · · · **Randomize, Rnd**
Get absolute value · · · · · · · · · · · · · · · · · · · · **Abs**
Get the sign of an expression · · · · · · · · · · · · **Sgn**
Numeric conversions · · · · · · · · · · · · · · · · · · **Fix, Int**
Trigonometry · · · · · · · · · · · · · · · · · · · · · · · · **Atn, Cos, Sin, Tan**

## Operators

Arithmetic · · · · · · · · · · · · · · · · · · · · · · · · · · **^, -, *, /, \**
· · · · · · · · · · · · · · · · · · · · · · · · · · · · · · · **Mod, +, &, =**
Comparison · · · · · · · · · · · · · · · · · · · · · · · · · **=, <>, <, >, <=**
· · · · · · · · · · · · · · · · · · · · · · · · · · · · · · · **>=, Like, Is**
Logical operations · · · · · · · · · · · · · · · · · · · · **Not, And, Or**
· · · · · · · · · · · · · · · · · · · · · · · · · · · · · · · **Xor, Eqv, Imp**

### Printing

| | |
|---|---|
| Control output appearance | **Scale, Spc, Tab** |
| | **TextHeight** |
| | **Text Width** |
| Control printer | **EndDoc, NewPage** |
| Print | **Print, PrintForm** |

### Procedures

| | |
|---|---|
| Call a Sub procedure | **Call** |
| Reference an external procedure | **Declare** |
| Define a procedure | **Function...End Function, Sub...End Sub** |
| Exit from a procedure | **Exit Function** |
| | **Exit Sub** |

### Strings

| | |
|---|---|
| Compare two strings | **StrComp** |
| Convert case | **Format, Lcase** |
| | **Ucase** |
| Create strings of repeating characters | **Space String** |
| Find the length of a string | **Len** |
| Format strings | **Format** |
| Justify a string | **LSet, RSet** |
| Manipulate strings | **InStr, Left, Ltrim** |
| | **Mid, Right, Rtrim** |
| | **Trim** |
| Set string comparison rules | **Option Compare** |
| Work with ASCII and ANSI values | **Asc, Chr** |

### Miscellaneous

| | |
|---|---|
| Automation | **CreateObject** |
| | **GetObject** |
| Colour | **QBColor, RGB** |
| Process pending events | **DoEvents** |
| Provide a command line string | **Command** |
| Run other programs | **AppActivate, Shell** |
| Send keystrokes to an application | **SendKeys** |
| Sound a beep | **Beep** |
| System | **Environ** |

**Registry**

| | |
|---|---|
| Delete program settings | **DeleteSetting** |
| Read program settings | **Get Setting** |
| | **GetAllSettings** |
| Save program settings | **SaveSetting** |

**Variables and Constants**

| | |
|---|---|
| Declare variables or constants | **Const, Dim, Private** |
| | **Public, New, Static** |
| Declare module as private | **Option Private** |
| | **Module** |
| Get information about a variant | **IsArray, IsDate** |
| | **IsEmpty, IsError** |
| | **IsMissing, IsNull** |
| | **IsNumeric, IsObject** |
| | **TypeName, VarType** |
| Refer to current object | **Me** |
| Require explicit variable declarations | **Option Explicit** |
| Set default data type | **Deftype** |

## Listed Alphabetically

Below is an alphabetic listing of Visual Basic's main function, statement and method key-words, with a short description of each. For more details of their use, look in the program Help.

**Abs** Function
Returns the absolute value of a number.

**AddItem** Method
Adds a new item to a list or combo box, or adds a new row to a grid control at run time.

**AddNew** Method
Clears the copy buffer in preparation for creating a new record in a Table or Dynaset.

**AppActivate** Statement
Activates an application window.

**Append** Method
Adds a new object to a collection.

**AppendChunk** Method
Appends data from a String to a Memo or Long Binary field in the copy buffer of a specified Table or Dynaset.

**Arrange** Method
Arranges the windows or icons within an MDI Form.

**Array** Function
Returns a Variant containing an array.

**Asc** Function
Returns a numeric value that is the ANSI code for the first character in a string expression.

**Atn** Function
Returns the arctangent of a number.

**Beep** Statement
Sounds a tone through the computer's speaker.

**BeginTrans** Statement
Begins a new transaction.

**Call** Statement
Transfers program control to a Visual Basic Sub procedure or a dynamic-link library (DLL) procedure.

**CCur** Function
Explicitly converts expressions to the Currency data type.

**CDbl** Function
Explicitly converts expressions to the Double data type.

**ChDir** Statement
Changes the current default directory on a specified drive.

**ChDrive** Statement
Changes the current drive.

**Choose** Function
Selects and returns a value from a list of arguments.

**CInt** Function
Explicitly converts expressions to the Integer data type.

**Chr, Chr$** Function
Returns a one-character string whose ANSI code is the argument.

**Circle** Method
Draws a circle, ellipse, or arc on an object.

**Clear** Method
Clears the contents of a list or combo box, or clears the contents of the operating environment Clipboard.

**Clone** Method
Returns a duplicate record set object that refers to the same record set from which it was created.

**CLng** Function
Explicitly converts expressions to the Long data type.

**Close** Method
Closes a specified Database, QueryDef, or record set.

**Cls** Method
Clears graphics and text generated at run time from a form or picture.

**Command, Command$** Function

Returns the argument portion of the command line used to launch Microsoft Visual Basic.

**CommitTrans** Statement

Transcends the current transaction.

**CompactDatabase** Statement

Compacts and encrypts or decrypts a Microsoft Access database.

**Const** Statement

Declares symbolic constants for use in place of values.

**Cos** Function

Returns the cosine of an angle (angle in radians).

**CreateDatabase** Function

Creates a Microsoft Access database, and returns a Database object that is open for exclusive read/write access.

**CreateDynaset** Method

Creates a Dynaset object from a specified Table object, QueryDef object, or SQL statement.

**CreateQueryDef** Method

Creates a new QueryDef in a specified database.

**CreateSnapshot** Method

Creates a Snapshot object from a specified table, QueryDef, or SQL statement.

**CSng** Function

Explicitly converts expressions to the Single data type.

**CStr** Function

Explicitly converts expressions to the String data type.

**CurDir, CurDir$** Function

Returns the current path for the specified drive.

**CVar** Function

Explicitly converts expressions to the Variant data type.

**CVDate** Function

Converts an expression to a Variant of VarType 7 (Date).

**Date, Date$** Functions
Returns the current system date.

**Date, Date$** Statement
Sets the current system date.

**DateAdd** Function
Returns a Variant containing a date to which a specified time interval has been added.

**DateDiff** Function
Returns a Variant containing the number of time intervals between two specified dates.

**DatePart** Function
Returns a specified part of a given date.

**DateSerial** Function
Returns the date serial for a specific year, month, and day.

**DateValue** Function
Returns the date represented by a String argument.

**Day** Method
Returns an integer between 1 and 31, inclusive, that represents the day of the month for a date argument.

**DDB** Function
Returns the depreciation of an asset for a specific period using the double-declining balance method.

**Declare** Statement
Declares references to external procedures in a dynamic-link library (DLL).

**DefInt** Statement
Sets the default data type as Integer.

**DefLng** Statement
Sets the default data type as Long.

**DefSng** Statement
Sets the default data type as Single.

**DefDbl** Statement
Sets the default data type as Double.

**DefStr** Statement
Sets the default data type as String.

**DefVar** Statement
Sets the default data type as Variant.

**Delete** Method
Deletes the current record in a specified Table or Dynaset.

**DeleteQueryDef** Method
Deletes a specified QueryDef from a database.

**Dim** Statement
Declares variables and allocates storage space.

**Dir, Dir$** Function
Returns the name of a file or directory that matches a specified pattern and file attribute.

**Do...Loop** Statement
Repeats a block of statements while a condition is true or until a condition becomes true.

**DoEvents** Function, **DoEvents** Statement
Causes Visual Basic to yield execution so that Windows can process events.

**Drag** Method
Begins, ends, or cancels dragging controls.

**Edit** Method
Opens the current record in a specified record set for editing by copying it to the copy buffer.

**End** Statement
Ends a Visual Basic procedure or block.

**EndDoc** Method
Terminates a document sent to the Printer, releasing it to the print device or spooler.

**Environ, Environ$** Function
Returns the string associated with an operating system environment variable.

**EOF** Function
> Returns a value during file input that indicates whether the end of a file has been reached.

**Erase** Statement
> Reinitialises the elements of fixed arrays and deallocates dynamic-array storage space.

**Err, Erl** Function
> Returns error status.

**Err** Statement
> Sets Err to a specific value.

**Execute** Method
> Invokes an action query in a specified database.

**ExecuteSQL** Method
> Executes an action query SQL statement in a specified database.

**Exit** Statement
> Exits a Do...Loop, a For...Next loop, a Function procedure, or a Sub procedure.

**Exp** Function
> Returns e (the base of natural logarithms) raised to a power.

**FieldSize** Method
> Returns the number of bytes in a text or binary field.

**FileAttr** Function
> Returns file mode or operating system file information about an open file.

**FileCopy** Statement
> Copies a file.

**FileDateTime** Function
> Returns a String that indicates the date and time a specified file was created or last modified.

**FileLen** Function
> Returns a Long integer that indicates the length of a file in bytes.

**FindFirst** Method
   Locates the first record that satisfies specified criteria and makes that record the current one.

**FindLast** Method
   Locates the last record that satisfies specified criteria and makes that record the current one.

**FindNext** Method
   Locates the next record that satisfies specified criteria and makes that record the current one.

**FindPrevious** Method
   Locates the previous record that satisfies specified criteria and makes that record the current one.

**Fix** Function
   Returns the integer portion of a number.

**For...Next** Statement
   Repeats a group of instructions a specified number of times.

**Format, Format$** Function
   Formats a number, date, time, or string according to instructions contained in a format expression.

**FreeFile** Function
   Returns the next valid unused file number.

**FreeLocks** Statement
   Suspends data processing, allowing a database to release locks on record pages and make all data in the local Dynaset objects current in a multi-user environment.

**Function** Statement
   Declares the name, arguments, and code that form the body of a Function procedure.

**FV** Function
   Returns the future value of an annuity based on periodic, constant payments and a constant interest rate.

**Get** Statement
   Reads from a disc file into a variable.

**GetAttr** Function

Returns an integer that indicates a file, directory, or volume label's attributes.

**GetChunk** Method

Returns all or a portion of a Memo or Long Binary field in a specified record set.

**GetData** Method

Returns a picture from the Clipboard object.

**GetFormat** Method

Returns an integer indicating whether there is an item in the Clipboard matching a specified format.

**GetText** Method

Returns a text string from the Clipboard.

**Global** Statement

Used in the Declarations section of a module to declare global variables and allocate storage space.

**GoSub...Return** Statement

Branch to, and return from, a subroutine within a procedure.

**GoTo** Statement

Branches to a specified line within a procedure.

**Hex, Hex$** Function

Returns a string that represents the hexadecimal value of a decimal argument.

**Hide** Method

Hides a form, but does not unload it.

**Hour** Function

Returns an integer between 0 and 23, inclusive, that represents the hour of the day corresponding to the time provided as an argument.

**If...Then...Else** Statement

Allows conditional execution, based on the evaluation of an expression.

**IIf** Function

Returns one of two parts depending on the evaluation of an expression.

**Input, Input$** Function
Reads characters from a sequential file.

**Input #** Statement
Reads data from a sequential file and assigns it to variables.

**InputBox, InputBox$** Function
Displays a prompt in a dialogue box and returns input from the user.

**InStr** Function
Returns the position of the first occurrence of one string within another string.

**Int** Function
Returns the integer portion of a number.

**IPmt** Function
Returns the interest payment for a given period of an annuity based on periodic, constant payments and a constant interest rate.

**IRR** Function
Returns the internal rate of return for a series of periodic cash flows.

**IsDate** Function
Returns a value indicating whether or not a Variant argument can be converted to a date.

**IsEmpty** Function
Returns a value indicating whether or not a Variant variable has been initialised.

**IsNull** Function
Returns a value that indicates whether or not a Variant contains the special Null value.

**IsNumeric** Function
Returns a value indicating whether or not a Variant variable can be converted to a numeric data type.

**Kill** Statement
Deletes file(s) from a disc.

**LBound** Function
Returns the smallest available subscript for the indicated dimension of an array.

**LCase, LCase$** Function
Returns a string in which all letters of an argument have been converted to lowercase.

**Left, Left$** Function
Returns the leftmost n characters of a string argument.

**Len** Function
Returns the number of characters in a string expression or the number of bytes required to store a variable.

**Let** Statement
Assigns the value of an expression to a variable.

**Line Input #** Statement
Reads a line from a sequential file into a String or Variant variable.

**Line** Method
Draws lines and rectangles on an object.

**LinkExecute** Method
Sends a command string to the other application in a dynamic data exchange (DDE) conversation.

**LinkPoke** Method
Transfers the contents of a control to the source application in a dynamic data exchange (DDE) conversation.

**LinkRequest** Method
Asks the source in a dynamic data exchange (DDE) conversation to update the contents of a control.

**LinkSend** Method
Transfers the contents of a picture control to the destination application in a dynamic data exchange (DDE) conversation.

**ListFields** Method
Creates a Snapshot with one record for each field in a specified record set.

**ListIndexes** Method
Creates a Snapshot with one record for each field in each index in a specified table.

**ListParameters** Method
Creates a Snapshot with one record for each parameter in a specified QueryDef object.

**ListTables** Method
Creates a Snapshot with one record for each Table or QueryDef in a specified database.

**Load** Statement
Loads a form or control into memory.

**LoadPicture** Function
Loads a picture into a form, picture box, or image control.

**Loc** Function
Returns the current position within an open file.

**Lock, Unlock** Statement
Controls access by other processes to an opened file.

**LOF** Function
Returns the size of an open file in bytes.

**Log** Function
Returns the natural logarithm of a number.

**LSet** Statement
Left aligns a string within the space of a string variable, or copies a variable of one user-defined type to another variable of a different user-defined type.

**LTrim, LTrim$** Function
Returns a copy of a string with leading spaces removed.

**Mid, Mid$** Function
Returns a string that is part of some other string.

**Mid, Mid$** Statement
Replaces part of a string with another string.

**Minute** Function
　　Returns an integer between 0 and 59, inclusive, that represents the minute of the hour corresponding to the time provided as an argument.

**MIRR** Function
　　Returns the modified internal rate of return for a series of periodic cash flows.

**MkDir** Statement
　　Creates a new directory.

**Month** Function
　　Returns an integer between 1 and 12, inclusive, that represents the month of the year for a date argument.

**Move** Method
　　Moves a form or control.

**MoveFirst, MoveLast, MoveNext, MovePrevious** Method
　　Moves to the first, last, next, or previous record in a specified record set and makes that record current.

**MsgBox** Function
　　Displays a message in a dialogue box, waits for the user to choose a button and returns a value indicating which button was pressed.

**MsgBox** Statement
　　Displays a message in a dialogue box and waits for the user to choose a button.

**Name** Statement
　　Changes the name of a disc file or directory.

**NewPage** Method
　　Ends the current page and advances to the next.

**Now** Function
　　Returns a date that represents the current date and time according to the computer's system clock.

**NPer** Function
　　Returns the number of periods for an annuity based on periodic, constant payments and a constant interest rate.

**NPV** Function

Returns the net present value of an investment based on a series of periodic cash flows and a discount rate.

**Oct, Oct$** Function

Returns text that represents the octal value of the decimal argument.

**On Error** Statement

Enables an error-handling routine and specifies the location of the routine within a procedure.

**On...GoSub, On...GoTo** Statement

Branches to one of several specified lines, depending on the value of an expression.

**Open** Statement

Enables input/output (I/O) to a file.

**OpenDatabase** Function

Opens an existing database and returns a Database object.

**OpenQueryDef** Method

Opens a specified QueryDef for editing.

**OpenTable** Method

Opens an existing table and returns a Table object.

**Option Base** Statement

Declares the default lower bound for array subscripts.

**Option Compare** Statement

Declares the default comparison mode to use when string data is compared.

**Option Explicit** Statement

Forces explicit declaration of all variables.

**Partition** Function

Returns a string indicating where a number occurs within a calculated series of ranges.

**Pmt** Function

Returns the payment for an annuity based on periodic, constant payments and a constant interest rate.

**Point** Method
Returns the RGB colour of the specified point on a form or picture box.

**PopupMenu** Method
Displays a pop-up menu on a form at the current mouse location, or at specified coordinates.

**PPmt** Function
Returns the principal payment for a given period of an annuity based on periodic, constant payments and a constant interest rate.

**Print #** Statement
Writes data to a sequential file.

**Print** Method
Prints a text string on an object using the current colour and font.

**PrintForm** Method
Sends a bit-for-bit image of a non-MDI form to the printer.

**PSet** Method
Sets a point on an object to a specified colour.

**Put** Statement
Writes from a variable to a disc file.

**PV** Function
Returns the present value of an annuity based on periodic, constant payments to be paid in the future and a constant interest rate.

**QBColor** Function
Returns the RGB colour code corresponding to a colour number.

**Randomize** Statement
Initialises the random-number generator.

**Rate** Function
Returns the interest rate per period for an annuity.

**ReDim** Statement
Used at the procedure level to declare dynamic-array variables and allocate or reallocate storage space.

**Refresh** Method
Forces an immediate update of a form, control, or object.

**RegisterDatabase** Statement
Makes connect information for an ODBC data source name available for use by the OpenDatabase function.

**Rem** Statement
Used to include explanatory remarks in a program.

**RemoveItem** Method
Removes an item from a list or combo box, or removes a row from a grid control, at run time.

**RepairDatabase** Statement
Attempts to repair a corrupted Microsoft Access database.

**Reset** Statement
Closes all disc files.

**Resume** Statement
Resumes program execution after an error-handling routine is finished.

**RGB** Function
Returns a long integer representing an RGB colour value.

**Right, Right$** Function
Returns the rightmost n characters of a string argument.

**RmDir** Statement
Removes an existing directory.

**Rnd** Function
Returns a random number, between 0 and 1.

**Rollback** Method
Ends the current transaction and restores the database to the state it was in when the transaction began.

**RSet** Statement
Right aligns a string within the space of a string variable.

**RTrim, RTrim$** Function
Returns a copy of a string with trailing (rightmost) spaces removed.

**SavePicture** Statement
Saves a picture from a form, picture box, or image control into a file.

**Scale** Method
Defines the co-ordinate system for an object.

**Second** Function
Returns an integer between 0 and 59, inclusive, that represents the second of the minute for a time argument.

**Seek** Function
Returns the current file position.

**Seek** Statement
Sets the position in a file for the next read or write operation.

**Select Case** Statement
Executes one of several statement blocks depending on the value of an expression.

**SendKeys** Statement
Sends one or more keystrokes to the active window as if they had been entered at the keyboard.

**Set** Statement
Assigns an object reference to a variable.

**SetAttr** Statement
Sets attribute information for a file.

**SetData** Method
Puts a picture in the Clipboard using the specified format.

**SetDataAccessOption** Statement
Sets a global option for data access usage.

**SetDefaultWorkspace** Statement
Establishes the user ID and password for protected (security-enabled) Microsoft Access databases.

**SetFocus** Method
Sets the focus to a form or control.

**SetText** Method

Puts a text string in the Clipboard using the specified Clipboard format.

**Sgn** Function

Returns an integer indicating the sign of a number.

**Shell** Function

Runs an executable program.

**Show** Method

Displays a form.

**Sin** Function

Returns the sine of an angle (angle in radians).

**SLN** Function

Returns the straight-line depreciation of an asset for a single period.

**Space, Space$** Function

Returns a string consisting of a specified number of spaces.

**Spc** Function

Skips a specified number of spaces in a Print # statement or Print method.

**Sqr** Function

Returns the square root of a number.

**Static** Statement

Used at the procedure level to declare variables and allocate storage space. Variables declared with the Static statement retain their value as long as the program is running.

**Stop** Statement

Suspends execution of the running Visual Basic code.

**Str, Str$** Function

Returns a string representation of the value of a numeric expression.

**StrComp** Function

Returns a Variant indicating the result of the comparison of two string arguments.

**String, String$ Function**
Returns a string whose characters all have a given ANSI code or are all the first character of a string expression.

**Sub Statement**
Declares the name, arguments, and code that form the body of a Sub procedure.

**Switch Function**
Evaluates a list of expressions and returns a value or an expression associated with the first expression in the list that is True.

**SYD Function**
Returns the sum-of-years' digits depreciation of an asset for a specified period.

**Tab Function**
Used with the Print # statement and the Print method to advance the print position.

**Tan Function**
Returns the tangent of an angle (angle in radians).

**TextHeight Method**
Returns the height of a text string as it would be printed in the current font of an object.

**TextWidth Method**
Returns the width of a text string as it would be printed in the current font of an object.

**Time, Time$ Function**
Returns the current system time.

**Time, Time$ Statement**
Sets the system time.

**Timer Function**
Returns the number of seconds that have elapsed since 12:00 a.m. (midnight).

**TimeSerial Function**
Returns the time serial for a specific hour, minute, and second.

**TimeValue** Function
Returns the time represented by a String argument.

**Trim, Trim$** Function
Returns a copy of a string with both leading and trailing spaces removed.

**Type** Statement
Defines a user-defined data type containing one or more elements.

**UBound** Function
Returns the largest available subscript for the indicated dimension of an array.

**UCase, UCase$** Function
Returns a string with all letters of an argument converted to uppercase.

**Unload** Statement
Unloads a form or control from memory.

**Update** Method
Saves the contents of the copy buffer to a specified Table or Dynaset.

**UpdateControls** Method
Gets the current record from a data control's record set and displays the appropriate data in controls bound to a data control.

**UpdateRecord** Method
Saves the current values of bound controls.

**Val** Function
Returns the numeric value of a string of characters.

**VarType** Function
Returns a value that indicates how a Variant is stored internally by Visual Basic.

**Weekday** Function
Returns an integer between 1 (Sunday) and 7 (Saturday) that represents the day of the week for a date argument.

**While...Wend** Statement
Executes a series of statements in a loop as long as a given condition is true.

**Width #** Statement
Assigns an output-line width to a file.

**Write#** Statement
Writes data to a sequential file.

**Year** Function
Returns an integer between 100 and 9999, inclusive, that represents the year of a date argument.

**ZOrder** Method
Places a specified form or control at the front or back of the z-order within its graphical level.

# Index

# Companion Discs

COMPANION DISCS are available for many of the computer books written by the same author(s) and published by BERNARD BABANI (publishing) LTD, as listed at the front of this book (except for those marked with an asterisk). These books contain many pages of file/program listings. There is no reason why you should spend hours typing them into your computer, unless you wish to do so, or need the practice.

## ORDERING INSTRUCTIONS

To obtain companion discs, fill in the order form below, or a copy of it, enclose a cheque (payable to **P.R.M. Oliver**) or a postal order, and send it to the address given below. **Make sure you fill in your name and address** and specify the book number and title in your order.

| Book No. | Book Name | Unit Price | Total Price |
|---|---|---|---|
| BP 498 | Using Visual Basic | £3.50 | |
| BP ........ | | £3.50 | |
| BP ........ | | £3.50 | |

| | | |
|---|---|---|
| Name  ............................. | Sub-total | £............. |
| Address ............................. | P & P (@ 45p/disc) | £............. |
| | | |
| | Total Due | £............. |

**Send to: P.R.M. Oliver, CSM, Pool, Redruth, Cornwall, TR SE**

**PLEASE NOTE**